Access to History

General Editor: Keith Randell

Henry VIII and the Government of England

Keith Randell

Hodder & Stoughton

A MEMBER OF THE HODDER HEADLINE GROUP

The cover illustration shows a copy of Holbein's portrait of Henry VIII (courtesy Walker Art Gallery, Liverpool)

Some other titles in the series:

Henry VII   ISBN 0 340 53801 5
Caroline Rogers

Henry VIII and the Reformation in England   ISBN 0 340 57805 X
Keith Randell

Edward VI and Mary: A Mid-Tudor Crisis?   ISBN 0 340 53560 1
Nigel Heard

Luther and the German Reformation, 1517–55   ISBN 0 340 51808 1
Keith Randell

Sweden and the Baltic, 1523–1721   ISBN 0 340 54644 1
Andrina Stiles

To Mary, without whom this book could not have been written

British Library Cataloguing in Publication Data
Randell, Keith
  Henry VIII and the government of England.
  – (Access to history)
  I. Title   II. Series
  942.05

  ISBN 0–340–55325–1

First published 1991
Impression number 10   9   8   7
Year   1998   1997

Typeset by Wearset, Boldon, Tyne and Wear
Printed in Great Britain for Hodder & Stoughton Educational, a division of Hodder Headline Plc, 338 Euston Road, London NW1 3BH by Redwood Books, Trowbridge, Wiltshire.

6.25

Access to History

Henry VIII and the
Government of England

Contents

Preface

To the general reader

Although the *Access to History* series has been designed with the needs of students studying the subject at higher examination levels very much in mind, it also has a great deal to offer the general reader. The main body of the text (i.e. ignoring the Study Guides at the ends of chapters) forms a readable and yet stimulating survey of a coherent topic as studied by historians. However, each author's aim has not merely been to provide a clear explanation of what happened in the past (to interest and inform): it has also been assumed that most readers wish to be stimulated into thinking further about the topic and to form opinions of their own about the significance of the events that are described and discussed (to be challenged). Thus, although no prior knowledge of the topic is expected on the reader's part, she or he is treated as an intelligent and thinking person throughout. The author tends to share ideas and possibilities with the reader, rather than passing on numbers of so-called 'historical truths'.

To the student reader

There are many ways in which the series can be used by students studying History at a higher level. It will, therefore, be worthwhile thinking about your own study strategy before you start your work on this book. Obviously, your strategy will vary depending on the aim you have in mind, and the time for study that is available to you.

If, for example, you want to acquire a general overview of the topic in the shortest possible time, the following approach will probably be the most effective:

1. Read Chapter 1 and think about its contents.
2. Read the 'Making notes' section at the end of Chapter 2 and decide whether it is necessary for you to read this chapter.
3. If it is, read the chapter, stopping at each heading or * to note down the main points that have been made.
4. Repeat stage 2 (and stage 3) where appropriate) for all the other chapters.

If, however, your aim is to gain a thorough grasp of the topic, taking however much time is necessary to do so, you may benefit from carrying out the same procedure with each chapter, as follows:

1. Read the chapter as fast as you can, and preferably at one sitting.
2. Study the flow diagram at the end of the chapter, ensuring that

you understand the general 'shape' of what you have just read.

3. Read the 'Making notes' section (and the 'Answering essay questions' section, if there is one) and decide what further work you need to do on the chapter. In particularly important sections of the book, this will involve reading the chapter a second time and stopping at each heading and * to think about (and to write a summary of) what you have just read.

4. Attempt the 'Source-based questions' section. It will sometimes be sufficient to think through your answers, but additional understanding will often be gained by forcing yourself to write them down.

When you have finished the main chapters of the book, study the 'Further Reading' section and decide what additional reading (if any) you will do on the topic.

This book has been designed to help make your studies both enjoyable and successful. If you can think of ways in which this could have been done more effectively, please write to tell me. In the meantime, I hope that you will gain greatly from your study of History.

Keith Randell

CHAPTER 1

Introduction: Henry VIII and the Government of England

> 1 Henry VIII was a strong King with a very strong sense of humour and VIII wives, memorable amongst whom were Katherine the Arrogant, Anne of Cloves, Lady Jane Austin and Anne Hathaway. His beard was, however, red.

So begins the chapter on 'Bluff King Hal' in Sellar and Yeatman's *1066 and All That*, a book that has enormously entertained history teachers and many of their pupils ever since its first publication in 1930. Although its lower school 'howler' style of humour works less well today than it did a generation ago, there are still plenty who appreciate it and who have enough basic 'knowledge' of British history to giggle at the deliberate mistakes.

With a subject such as Henry VIII, Sellar and Yeatman were on particularly safe ground because there can be very few people who have been through the British education system up to the age of 14 who have not carried away with them some memory of this larger than life king and his many wives. Few readers of these words will not bring to the study of this book powerful preconceptions about the character who is at the centre of it – many of them probably unrecognised.

Now is the time to examine such preconceptions and, if possible, to discard them. It will be difficult enough to formulate coherent opinions about the man who reigned (and many would say ruled) in England from 1509 to 1547 when approaching the subject with an open mind. Readers with firmly established expectations about what they will find, will be faced with an almost impossible task. Prior knowledge of indisputable facts can only be an advantage, but a supposed understanding of the patterns that these facts make is likely to be highly inhibiting to new thinking. If it cannot be put to one side at the outset of a student's work on this topic, it should at least be consciously recognised and no attempt should be made to fit what follows into its framework. To do so would be to waste a marvellous opportunity to reach fresh and independent conclusions about this remarkable man and his reign.

1 Henry and his Six Wives

Almost everybody knows about Henry VIII and his six wives. It is an integral part of British folk lore.

> Divorced, beheaded, died,
> divorced, beheaded, survived.

is a jingle that tens of thousands of school children have memorised in preparation for a test on the key facts of Henry's reign. It has been very useful for this purpose, but it seems to have had the unintended side-effect of suggesting that there was a particular pattern to Henry's marital history which there was not.

For most of his adult life (from 1509 to 1533) Henry was married to the same person – Catherine of Aragon, a daughter of Ferdinand and Isabella whose own marriage had united all of the Iberian kingdoms, except Portugal, to form the new country of Spain. Catherine (so spelt by a mysterious modern convention, despite the fact that contemporaries almost universally began it with a 'K') was in almost all respects a model wife judged by the standards of the time. She was dignified yet dutiful, rejoiced in her husband's attentiveness but was uncomplaining about his indiscretions, and played the part of the seemly consort to perfection in both public and private. She created a positive impression on all who met her, in the process acquiring many friends and admirers but no real enemies. She even obliged her husband with a steady stream of pregnancies. It is true that some of these miscarried, but at least five of them resulted in live births. However, only one of these (Mary) survived for long. The others, including three sons, died within hours or days, and this was her undoing. By the early 1520s it was established beyond any doubt that she would bear no more children. Henry thus became painfully aware that while the marriage continued he was certain to be denied one of his most fervent desires – male heirs to continue the Tudor dynasty. Although he already had one illegitimate son whom he created the Duke of Richmond and whom he seemed to be grooming to succeed him, he knew in his heart of hearts that his subjects would be unlikely to accept such an arrangement once he was dead and no longer able to enforce it.

As the years passed Henry's concern about his lack of legitimate sons became an obsession. Added to this, he became captivated by Anne Boleyn, a woman who refused to yield her honour to him until he was in a position to marry her. He therefore became determined that his marriage ties with Catherine must be broken – and an ideal excuse appeared to be available. Catherine had first been married to Henry's elder brother (Arthur), and a plausible argument could be advanced that the Bible forbade remarriages of a man with his brother's widow. However, it took seven years and the beginnings of a revolution (issues discussed in detail in *Henry VIII and the Reformation in England* in this series) for Henry and Catherine's marriage to be annulled by a court that most Englishmen were prepared to accept as competent to deal with the issue.

At last (in 1533) the king was free to marry a woman young enough to offer him the prospect of bearing many children. But Anne Boleyn was a disappointment in this respect. Although she was already pregnant at the time of her marriage, the resulting offspring (a daughter, Elizabeth) was to be her only successful experience of child-bearing. In 1536 'Anne of a Thousand Days' was found guilty on spurious charges of adultery with, among others, her brother, and was executed. Her husband was thereby freed to enter a third partnership in his increasingly desperate attempt to sire a son who would survive into adulthood.

Jane Seymour was not only able to face the world as the undisputed Queen of England – Catherine of Aragon having died of natural causes shortly before Anne Boleyn met her less peaceful end – but she was also successful at her first attempt in the 'maternal stakes'. In 1537 she gave birth to the future Edward VI. But she paid for her triumph with her life, dying of the effects of childbirth a few days later. Thereafter, Henry's matrimonial affairs assumed a large element of farce. Although Edward's survival beyond the dangerous early weeks removed most of the panic from the situation, both the king and his leading minister (Thomas Cromwell) believed that there were diplomatic and dynastic advantages to be gained from a well-chosen fourth marriage. The fact that Henry insisted on seeing portraits of all the potential brides (once the King of France had declined to arrange 'a parade' of the leading contenders at Calais on the grounds that to do so would be unseemly) strongly suggests that he still thought of his own *alliances* in terms of personal satisfaction, which he had singularly failed to do when arranging the marriages of others.

For some now unfathomable reason Henry took an immediate dislike to Cromwell's preferred (on diplomatic grounds) candidate – Anne, the 34-year-old daughter of the ruler of the strategically placed dukedom of Cleves (see the map on page 27). Dishonestly flattering reports and a less than accurate portrait were used by Cromwell to win his master's agreement to the match, but the prospective bridegroom's doubts remained. These became certainties once he set eyes on his bride-to-be and found that (seemingly without good reason) her looks repelled him. It took all Cromwell's skill as a persuader – allied to a realisation of the dire diplomatic consequences that might have resulted had he given offence to England's potential protestant allies at a time when it looked as if a coalition of catholic states might be about to invade the country to restore the pope's authority – to convince Henry that it was not practical for him to withdraw from his commitment to Anne of Cleves at such a late stage. So the wedding went ahead (in January 1540), but the king had already determined that he would never consummate his marriage to this 'Flanders mare'. Nor did he. Instead, Cromwell was disgraced and executed – partly because of the matrimonial embarrassment his policy had caused – while later in the year Anne contentedly accepted the annulment of a marriage she had not welcomed, together with a sizeable financial settlement which allowed her to live the quiet life she sought, free from the danger of being used as a pawn in the international game of political and dynastic marriage-making.

Henry's fifth marriage, to Catherine Howard in 1540, was a clear case of 'old man's folly'. His passion was enflamed by a flighty young *protégé* of one of the court factions and he allowed himself to be manoeuvred into marrying her. Unfortunately the new queen had little common sense and less discretion. She soon provided her political enemies with the evidence that she had at least seriously contemplated adultery, which was sufficient grounds for a charge of treason to be levelled against her. She was executed in 1542.

By now Henry had given up hope of fathering further sons, and all his hopes rested on the frail health of Edward. However, in the year following Catherine Howard's execution he married yet again. This time his choice fell upon the twice-widowed Catherine Parr, who provided him with just the quality of level-headed care and concern that was needed in the king's ailing years. Whether or not her qualities of good housewifery were recognised before she became queen is not known. But whether by luck or by judgement, Henry's last foray into matrimony was a success and his need for quiet companionship and devout solace was well met.

2 The Changing Interests of Historians

Although the story of Henry VIII and the women in his life yielded writers with fascinating copy well into the twentieth century – and film and television directors with irresistible material as late as the 1960s – professional historians have long attempted to balance the writing of compelling narrative with a search for wider significance. By the second half of the nineteenth century it was commonplace for the importance of Henry's reign to be debated in academic circles. As a result, during the last century and a half a bewildering range of issues from the years 1509 to 1547 has been unearthed as being worthy of historical debate. There are so many of them that they could not all be adequately aired in even a small collection of books the size of the current volume. However, two general strands of inquiry are discernible, although they are a long way from being either self-contained or all-embracing. The first has to do with religion and the issues that are intimately linked with it. This is the subject of the companion volume *Henry VIII and the Reformation in England* in this series.

The second strand may conveniently be labelled 'political'. This has two *foci*: a long-running debate on the personality and character of the king, including a consideration of the part he played in the politics of his time; and an assessment of the significance of the reign in the long-term political development of the country variously described as England, Britain and the United Kingdom – normally depending on the author's ability to distance him/herself intellectually from London! This is the strand on which this book concentrates.

The dispute over Henry's personality has been running since the early seventeenth century and it shows no sign of abating. For most of this time writers have tended to take up extreme positions. They have either seen him as a wicked tyrant, possibly with a few redeeming features, or have portrayed him as the 'Bluff King Hal' who was a cross between Father Christmas and John Bull, although he was sometimes forced to take actions that 'were not quite nice'. For example, Sir Walter Raleigh, one of the earliest authors to pass general comment in print, was in no doubt where he stood.

1 Now for King Henry the eight: if all the pictures and patterns of a merciless prince were lost in the world, they might be again painted to the life out of the story of this king.

In recent decades, following a rash of one-dimensional semi-psychological biographies between the First and Second World Wars, writers have attempted to present a more balanced picture, leaving the reader with the impression that Henry was a complex mixture of 'good' and 'evil'. However, this seeming blurring of the old battle lines is misleading. With a little care it is possible to detect in even more recent writers an underlying stance on Henry the man that permeates their work. For each commentator Henry is basically either good or strong, with strands of evil or weakness, or bad or weak, with elements of virtue or strength. It seems that there is no way in which this fundamental judgement can be avoided. Many would add, 'nor should it be'. Certainly, any thinking reader of the chapters that follow would be hard pressed not to join one side or the other. Chapter 2 seeks to establish the issue directly, and all the other chapters reflect on it at least obliquely. Chapters 5 and 7 come closest to being case studies of the subject, but it is expected that each reader will attempt to use all that follows to help formulate a personal answer to the question, 'What sort of man was Henry VIII?'.

Henry had two outstanding political servants – sometimes described as first ministers – during his reign. Up to 1529 there was Thomas Wolsey (from 1515 normally known as Cardinal Wolsey) and in the 1530s there was Thomas Cromwell (no relation to Oliver Cromwell, one of the leading political figures of the seventeenth century). Twentieth-century historians have disagreed violently about the extent to which the servants controlled their master and the degree to which it is valid to think of them as operating policies of their own. Chapters 3 and 4 concentrate on Cardinal Wolsey, while chapter 6 discusses Cromwell. But because both men (and especially Cromwell) were deeply involved in the Reformation in England, full coverage of their contributions will not be available in this book alone – although it should be possible to

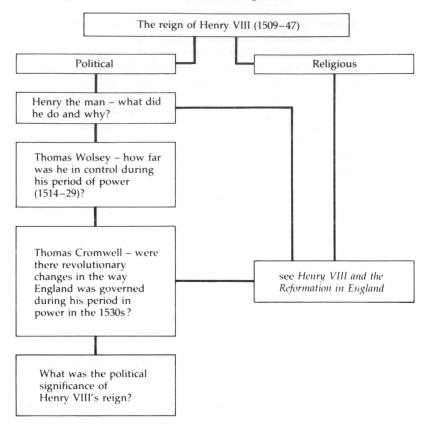

Summary – Introduction: Henry VIII and the Government of England

obtain a fairly 'rounded' view of Wolsey from pages 32–69.

It is hardly surprising that each generation of historians has tended to assess the significance of Henry's reign in terms of the issues that were 'live' in their own time. Thus, during the later part of the nineteenth and the first decades of the twentieth centuries, when English (or British?) nationalism was strong and when Britannia ruled the waves, the concentration was on the contribution that Henry made to the creation of a more united and totally independent kingdom and to the establishment of a navy. Because more research has cast doubt on whether significant progress was made in either respect before the reign of Elizabeth I, these issues are now of little more than historiographical interest, and will not be considered further in the following chapters.

Much more important is the debate started by Sir Geoffrey (then G. R.) Elton in the early 1950s. He identified the reign of Henry VIII, and more specifically the 1530s under the influence of Thomas

Cromwell, as the time when revolutionary changes took place in the way England was governed. His claim was that the period marked the transition from medieval to modern forms of government, which was only paralleled in importance in British history by the changes that took place in the middle of the nineteenth century. Such was the brilliance and freshness of Elton's work (which he continued to build on for more than 30 years) that few historians of the period have subsequently been able to distance themselves from the storm of controversy that has swirled around the issue ever since. A consideration of some of the questions raised by Elton's work provides the framework for chapter 6.

While the Elton controversy was at its height some historians also developed an argument that the final years of Henry's reign were of significance because they ushered in a 20 year period of instability in England that they termed 'the mid-Tudor crisis'. This issue is dealt with directly in Nigel Heard's *Edward VI and Mary: A Mid-Tudor Crisis?* in this series. The topic will, therefore, only be touched on briefly in this book.

Studying 'Introduction: Henry VIII and the Government of England'

As you work on this topic you will, no doubt, learn a large number of facts (especially names and dates). In practice, you may well end up memorising much of the *Chronological Table* on pages 144–6. But this will be a by-product rather than the main thrust of your endeavour, because your aims in studying the reign of Henry VIII will need to be stated in terms of 'historically significant issues'.

Your first task will be to identify these. This should be relatively easy to do if you re-read the second section of this chapter, although your definitions of them will be expanded and clarified as a result of your work on the rest of this book.

Your second task will be the most time-consuming. You need to understand as much as you can about each issue. This will involve finding out why historians consider it to be significant, the nature of the disagreements there have been over its interpretation, and the main pieces of evidence that can be used to support the various points of view. It is as you carry out this task that you are likely to learn most of the factual information you will require.

Your third task is by far the most difficult, and you may even find it preferable to leave it until you are undertaking your major review of the topic towards the end of your course. The task is reaching your own conclusions about each of the issues you have identified and studied. This need not be as daunting as it may seem at first sight because no-one is expecting you to rival the professional historians in either expertise or the ability to think analytically about the topic. All that is hoped for is that you will often be able to support one point of view rather than another, and that you will be able to explain why you have come to the conclusion you have. However, it may sometimes be that all the interpretations you encounter seem plausible and that you feel you have insufficient evidence to judge between them. This is a totally acceptable stance for you to take – as long as you are able to offer a justification for your decision in each case – because it is sometimes better to 'sit on the fence' over complex matters and to admit honestly that the evidence is not conclusive. In fact, this may often be the most sensible course of action with contentious historical issues where the surviving evidence is both partial and open to various interpretations. 'Historical uncertainty' is an integral part of any study of the subject: it is not an automatic sign of weakness. This is why historians use so many qualifying words – such as 'possibly', 'probably', and 'seemingly' – when recording their conclusions. You will be well advised to follow their example.

Many students dislike making notes – and not just because, like Henry VIII, they find the act of writing uncongenial. Others copy out page upon page of factual information in the belief that there is virtue in doing so. But it is the commendable exception who 'teases out' his or her own ideas about an issue by writing them down. This is because it is painful to do so – it involves a lot of thinking. Yet, these are the most valuable type of notes to make, and it is well worth making the effort to write an analytical account of what you have read, even if you seem to be spending much longer thinking than writing! You will have plenty of opportunity to put this advice into practice as you work on the chapters that follow.

CHAPTER 2

Henry VIII, the Man and the King

1 The New King

On 21 April 1509 Henry VIII became King of England at the age of 17 years and 10 months. Most of those who have left a written record of their opinion at the time saw the change of monarch as a dawning of a new age. Thomas More wrote a Latin poem that was presented to Henry at his coronation. It contained the statement that:

1 This day is the end of our slavery, the fount of our liberty; the end of sadness and the beginning of joy.

The contrast between the dead king and his successor could hardly have been more pronounced (see the illustration on page 10). In his final years Henry VII had looked and lived like a mean old man. He had rarely appeared in public and had been best known for the way he extracted money from the wealthier of his subjects by dubious means. He had been feared because of the financial penalties he could exact, but he had not been widely respected. His son, in clear contrast, was young, energetic and accessible, and with a very obvious joy in living and in being king. He spent money with an abandon and a lack of forethought that matched popular expectations of how the mighty should conduct themselves. As if to stress that all had changed, he almost immediately took two very public decisions which announced that it was 'out with the old and in with the new'. Edmund Dudley and Sir Richard Empson, the two men who had been most responsible for implementing Henry VII's policy of the financial intimidation of his leading subjects, were arrested and imprisoned in the Tower, later to be executed. And it was made known that Catherine of Aragon was to become the new queen. The latter decision was generally seen to be a chivalrous action towards an obviously virtuous young woman who, through no fault of her own, had for seven years been used by the old king as a pawn in his complex diplomatic manoeuvrings. During this time (since she had been widowed by the death of Arthur, Henry VII's eldest son) her ex-father-in-law had refused either to return her to her parents, along with her dowry, as should have been done, or to marry her to his second son as he had periodically promised to do. As a result, Catherine had become a virtual prisoner in a foreign land, and had won widespread admiration by the dignified way in which she had conducted herself throughout her adversity. The new king's decision was interpreted as a conscious attempt to put right the wrongs of the past.

But, startling as the change of monarchs was, it would be sensible to exercise caution in accepting the statements of contemporaries at their

Henry VIII and Henry VII – Holbein's working drawing

face value. Not only is it likely that some of them were lured into exaggeration by their enthusiasm about what they imagined would be the consequences of the accession of a promising young king, but it was also customary for monarchs to be written about in glowing terms, whether or not the facts justified the statements. To do so was a literary convention of the age, even in writings that were intended to be only for private consumption. This is made very clear by what was written about other rulers who are known to have been very 'ordinary', and by the accounts of Henry in later life when other evidence proves that he was anything but the stately and dignified figure he was often claimed to be. What was often being described was the glory that was meant to be an integral part of royalty, rather than the reality that the witness was observing. However, this is not to suggest that the flattering descriptions of the young Henry should be totally discounted, but rather that they should be regarded as possibilities for which corroborative evidence needs to be sought.

2 Henry the Man

Henry VIII was king for more than 37 years. During this time he both matured and aged. Certainly, he did not remain the same. In some things he changed as a result of his experiences or of the passage of years: in others he became more entrenched as his confidence grew and as some of the uncertainties and flexibilities of youth disappeared with the progression through middle to, what was for the period, old age. Thus, over the course of his entire reign he was that mixture of constancy and change, consistency and contradiction that should realistically be expected of most people. So it should not be expected that the question, 'What sort of man was Henry VIII?' could be answered in simple or unqualified terms. At the very least, the question 'when?' should always be in the answerer's mind.

a) Appearance and Physique

It is self-evident that provisos about date should always be present when commenting on the looks of a historical figure. It is normal to contrast the young Henry with the aging king of the final years and to assume that his life saw a steady progression from one state to the other. The stages by which the change took place are not well documented, but what is not in doubt is that the 17-year-old who became king was a young man with considerable physical attributes and that the 55-year-old who died repulsed most of those who saw him.

Judgement of looks, of course, is a matter of taste which varies from society to society and from time to time. For us it may be difficult fully to reconcile the contemporary opinion that the young Henry was 'extremely handsome, nature could not have done more for him; . . .

Henry VIII in early manhood

very fair, and his whole frame admirably proportioned' with the
portrait above. Perhaps 'striking' would be the most appropriate way of
describing the king during the early years of his adult life.

The visual impact Henry made for much of his reign was largely the
result of his fine physique. He was tall, large-framed, well proportioned
and very muscular. In fact, he well-deserved the modern description of
being 'a bull of a man'. And he knew how to make the best of his
physical attributes. He carried himself well and he paid great attention
to the clothes he wore. A foreign observer described him as 'the best

dressed sovereign in the world'. His most famous portrait (reproduced on the front cover) illustrates well both his physique and the use he made of it. It also hints strongly at the enormous pride he took in his appearance.

b) Interests

Henry was first and foremost a sportsman. Not only in his youth, but also well into middle age, his greatest love was competitive physical activity. Hunting on horseback was what he enjoyed most. The activity was essentially a race between a group of companions to reach the quarry (preferably a stag or a wild boar) first. Several changes of horse would normally be needed as the chase could go on for several hours and the pursuit made great physical demands of all concerned. Henry was rarely found wanting. In fact, he would probably have been the 'winner' on most occasions, even had his associates not been tactful enough to ensure that he was. A possibly exaggerated contemporary account reported that he never went hunting:

1 without tiring eight or ten horses, which he causes to be stationed beforehand along the line of the country he may mean to take, and when one is tired, he mounts another, and before he gets home they are all exhausted.

When he was young, an early version of tennis was also one of his special favourites. He was very good at it, although his style of play, as much as the results he gained, clearly impressed onlookers. However, the following comment is perhaps more revealing of its author than of the king!

1 He is extremely fond of tennis, at which game it is the prettiest thing in the world to see him play, his fair skin glowing through the shirt of the finest texture.

Undoubtedly the most publicly visible of Henry's sporting activities was jousting. This was thought to be the true sport of kings and, although there was an immense amount of play-acting and ceremony involved, the act of charging on heavily armoured horses in an attempt to unseat an opponent with a lance was highly dangerous for the participants. This was despite the fact that they were theoretically well protected by full suits of armour, the survival of which has allowed historians to chart the king's steadily increasing girth! Henry began his jousting career soon after he ascended the throne and he continued it for 25 years. In the process he established and maintained a reputation as a fine athlete – besides being very nearly killed on one occasion. It has even been argued that the accident that finally persuaded him to hang up his spurs in 1536 left him permanently brain damaged (see page 114). Because it was a brave (or foolhardy) man who allowed himself to emerge victorious in any sporting contest with his monarch, it is impossible to reach any conclusions about the extent to which Henry excelled as an athlete, but it seems likely that he would (in his prime) have been able to hold his own on equal terms with all but the best in the land. Otherwise, some of his less intelligent companions would surely have failed to lose as regularly as they did!

It has sometimes been assumed that a man who was sport-mad and who married six times must also have been blessed (or punished) with a strong sex-drive. However, it seems that this was not so in Henry's case. In fact, he was probably more interested in the romantic side of love-making than in its physical aspects. He had fewer mistresses and fewer illegitimate children (probably only two) than most male rulers of his time, and he was prepared to wait six years for Anne Boleyn, the major passion of his life, to surrender to his sexual advances. However, this is not to suggest, as some writers have done, that his virility was questionable. It is merely to argue that Henry was in no sense the sexual predator that he has sometimes popularly been made out to be. But this was not because he had any moral objection to promiscuity, or any belief that he should be faithful to his wife of the moment. He was just not very interested in women. In fact, some historians have claimed that he viewed them as little more than child-bearing machines.

Yet if his sexual appetite needed infrequent satisfaction, his love of food and drink was huge and abiding. He ate and drank enormous quantities on a regular basis and was fortunate to survive the effects for so long. But it should be remembered that his gluttony was typical of his class at the time (and for centuries to come), for the concept of excessive eating did not then exist. It was assumed that those who were rich enough to be able to afford huge quantities of food – especially meat – would have been silly to deny themselves such obvious and seemingly harmless pleasures. The age of 'sensible eating' was yet to dawn, and those who survived into their forties and fifties, if well-to-do, were expected to be of a size that announced to the world that they were rich enough to afford what they liked. Henry was not unique in ending up with a body that was too heavy for his legs to support.

It is clear that all of Henry's life-long interests were physical. But he was capable of being temporarily enthused by an extended range of activities. As he liked to think of himself as a true Renaissance man, adept at all the pastimes (loosely termed 'cultural') that were known to have flourished in ancient Greece and Rome, he was prepared to make the effort required to become a competent musician and a passable scholar. And if the songs that have survived as his were really created by him, his accomplishment was of a reasonably high order. The same is true of his theological scholarship. However, the suspicion is that, although the conceptions may have been his, any hard work was done by others. Certainly he made no secret of the fact that, as an adult, he found both reading and writing (even the signing of his name) to be laborious and that he avoided them completely, as far as possible.

c) Intellectual Abilities

Those who wished to ingratiate themselves with Henry were almost certain of success if they told him that he was very clever. This was because the king prided himself on the quality of his mind. And he was right to do so, because he appeared able to think his way around complicated issues almost as well as the most able of his subjects. It has even been suggested that the favour he extended to men of outstanding ability (at least until he believed that they had betrayed him) such as the three Thomases – Wolsey, More and Cromwell – was probably based on the fact that they could (unusually) function at his intellectual level.

Contemporary writings contain many references to his intellectual powers. Even when the exaggeration is stripped away from verdicts such as those that describe him as having 'exceptional and almost more than human talents', and the judgement of Erasmus, the arch-flatterer of the early sixteenth century, that, as a child, he had possessed 'a vivid and active mind, above measure able to execute whatever tasks he undertook . . . You would say he was a universal genius', there is reason to believe that he should be numbered among the gifted. But, of course, it is the way he performed during the 37 years of his reign that offers the most reliable evidence of his relative intellectual ability. And the picture is clear. He could, and regularly did, out-think all members of the English aristocracy. He was also personally more than a match for the other leading rulers of western Europe, although, of course, not necessarily for their advisers. His mind may not have been as well trained as those of some of his most able subjects, but this was hardly surprising given his lack of formal educational training. Nevertheless, he could both appreciate the strengths and spot the weaknesses of any argument that was laid before him, however skilful the presentation. As a result it was almost impossible for 'the wool to be pulled over his eyes' – at least, for long. On the few occasions when he was hoodwinked by those who advised him – as over the supposed treacheries of Cardinal Wolsey, Anne Boleyn and Thomas Cromwell – it was his emotions rather than his intellect that were persuaded, and then only after concerted campaigns of suppressing evidence and perverting the facts. Even the best minds reach incorrect conclusions if they are persistently fed with false information! Although there is no scientifically valid evidence available to support the contention, it is probable that Henry VIII was the most academically able monarch in English history.

d) Values and Attitudes

Henry was a conformist. It is, therefore, not surprising that he adopted and retained most of the values and attitudes of his sex, his class and his age. His assumption that women were inferior to men was deeply ingrained and was only temporarily suspended for brief periods during his relationship with Anne Boleyn. Anne was a remarkable person in many respects, but especially in her refusal to be treated as a second-class citizen because of her gender. However, for most of his life Henry treated women like chattels and was swift to remind any female who did not 'know her place' that subservience was expected of her. His anger at Catherine of Aragon for refusing to accept being 'put aside' with a good grace was never assuaged and largely explains why he celebrated her death with public relish in 1536. He was equally affronted when his daughter Mary refused to accept the bastardy that resulted from the annulment of her parents' marriage, and was only prepared to return her to his favour when she promised to accept his authority in all matters unreservedly in future. It can even be maintained that Anne Boleyn's final undoing, resulting in her execution, was made possible only because the king's dislike of her precosity eventually became stronger than the fascination she exercised over him. Certainly a large part of the last affection that Henry felt for Jane Seymour, which long survived her death following the birth of their son (later Edward VI) in 1537, resulted from the fact that she fully accepted her husband's views about the inferiority of women. Equally, Anne of Cleves not only survived but also flourished following the rapid dissolution of her marriage with Henry because she was prepared to accept the king's will without demur. Even the more personable Catherine Parr was able to survive a concerted effort to remove her (see page 124) by throwing herself unreservedly on her husband's mercy and by declaring that she wished to follow his instructions in every detail.

Just as Henry unthinkingly accepted the prevailing attitudes about the hierarchical relationship between the sexes, so he was also unquestioning about the validity of the existing social hierarchy. He accepted that God had ordered society as it then was and that it was a sin for anyone to challenge the place he or she had been assigned within it. As did almost all of those around him, he assumed that not only morality, but also the preservation of civilisation as he understood it, depended on the maintenance of existing social distinctions. He, therefore, behaved ruthlessly towards any groups or individuals who dared to endanger the prevailing order of things (see chapter 5).

The value that Henry attached to human life and human suffering was similarly in line with the prevailing orthodoxy. This was that the time spent on earth was merely a brief interlude in the soul's eternal life. Whether it was lengthened or shortened by a few years, or made more or less painful by the use of, for example, judicial torture was therefore of minimal importance in the wider scheme of things. Given this scale of values, it would have indeed been surprising had he felt any sustained guilt or sorrow about the thousands of premature deaths for which he was probably directly responsible. Many would argue that this did not make him an ogre, as he was merely acting according to the accepted standards of his time.

Henry differed from his father in his attitude towards self-discipline and endeavour. But Henry VII, with his insistence on working on the detail of governing his kingdom, had been atypical and had been despised (if feared) by most of his leading subjects for failing to live up to popular expectations of how a ruler should conduct himself. There was no danger that Henry VIII would fall into the same trap. He happily accepted that work was generally something that was done by servants, while masters devoted their time to activities that better befitted their status. In the case of kings this was performing grand deeds, whether in court, sport or battle. It was acceptable to strive mightily in such endeavours, but other affairs were to be taken lightly and with studied casualness. If servants were well chosen, their supervision should require a minimum of effort. They would undertake whatever smacked of 'business' once the desired direction in which affairs should move had been made clear to them. The same principles underlie the Hindu cast system, although here they have been taken closer to their logical conclusion. In early sixteenth-century western Europe the distinctions were not nearly so hard and fast. As a result, Henry was able to apply himself diligently from time to time to the *minutiae* of kingship without endangering his regal reputation.

e) Beliefs

Henry was a man with strong beliefs that remained largely unchanged throughout his adult life. He seemingly never doubted either the existence or the nature of the Christian God, nor the detail of what this deity expected of him. There seems to have been little that could be described as spiritual in his beliefs. It appears that Henry thought of God as a sort of super-man, sitting on a throne somewhere in the sky, from where he could observe all that was happening on earth and be ready to reward or punish those who followed or broke his commandments. It also seems that Henry believed that his position as a king empowered him to make special deals with God whenever the need arose.

As a child Henry had been brought up to believe that his role in life was to be a 'true knight' according to the code of chivalry which had been developed at the Burgundian court in the Netherlands during the previous century and which had been given a particularly English flavour by the widespread re-telling of the legends about King Arthur and the Knights of the Round Table. One important aspect of this code was the need for men to perform 'valiant deeds'. These could be in ceremonial form – by partaking in jousting or in the elaborate mock battles that were sometimes staged as grand court spectacles – but in their highest form they could only be undertaken in real-life warfare, where the risks and the rewards were genuine. As it seems that he had also been repeatedly told the story of his namesake-predecessor, Henry V, who, less than a hundred years previously, had earned eternal glory by winning a great victory at Agincourt against the French and by securing the crown of France for the English royal family, it is hardly surprising that Henry entered manhood believing that his destiny was to perform similar deeds of valour on the far side of the Channel.

Closely associated with the martial aspect of chivalry was the concept of 'courtly love'. A 'true knight' was not expected to perform valiantly on the field of battle in order to win wealth or worldly power (although these might naturally follow a victory), but so that he would have worthwhile trophies to lay at the feet of his 'fair lady'. The woman he thus served might be his own wife, might be unattached or might even be the wife of another. In any case, no impropriety would be involved and (hopefully) no offence given, because there need be no physical contact, beyond the possible kissing of a hand, between a knight and the recipient of his 'love'. The relationship was one that was meant to represent romance in its purest form – a knight carrying out disinterested service for a lady. Evidence of Henry's attachment to this code as a young man abounds, not only in the way he treated Catherine of Aragon at jousts and court festivities, but in the way he hurried back to her to present her with the symbols of his victorious campaign in France in 1513. Although the king seems to have become less enamoured with such conventions when he passed out of his twenties, (the Field of Cloth of Gold in 1520 was the last of Henry's great chivalric extravaganzas – see page 36), they certainly continued to flourish among the younger members of his court. Even as late as 1536 Anne Boleyn acted as the 'fair lady' for several young men, a willingness that was made the basis of the charges of adultery that were fatally levelled against her.

However much Henry cooled towards the romance of chivalry, there was one aspect of the code that remained central to his beliefs throughout his life. This was the concept of honour. His initial approach to most issues was shaped by his understanding of this concept – that kings should always be obeyed and that they should never be under the influence of others. It would hardly be an exaggeration to claim that all his public actions and all his reactions to the doings of others were initially planned by Henry in terms of their effect upon his honour. The documents he left behind him and the reports that survive of his explanations of his actions strongly support this contention. 'What was the honourable way in which a king should act?', and 'Was the action reported to him an affront to his honour?', were the questions that he most frequently asked himself when considering what he should do.

f) Personality and Character

Historians have disagreed radically about what sort of man Henry was. The controversy has been over whether he was fundamentally strong or basically weak; whether he was the puppet or the puppeteer. No lasting consensus has emerged and the issue is likely to be argued over into the foreseeable future. The problem is that there is sufficient evidence to allow a persuasive case to be made for both points of view, but not enough to prove one or the other conclusively. While each writer can rationalise the position he or she takes up, the decision on which 'side' to support is usually made according to that indefinable attribute we call 'feel'.

It would be fair to say that the majority of the current generation of leading researchers have concluded that Henry was essentially strong. Their view has been that he possessed sufficient determination, self-assurance, intellectual ability, and political shrewdness to ensure that the conduct of public life in his kingdom and in its dealings with other states followed the lines that he determined (in as far as any individual can meaningfully control the course of events). They accept that he frequently allowed his leading servants, especially Wolsey, considerable scope for independent action, but that he always retained control of the direction of policy and was fully able to assume the detailed direction of events whenever he wished. They also admit that he was periodically weak and indecisive, especially in the latter part of his reign when severe pain sometimes sapped his resolve, but they maintain that such occasions were the exceptions rather than the rule. Their overall contention is that Henry did not only appear to be the colossus who dominated affairs in his domains, but that such was essentially the reality of the situation. Thus they maintain that the king made use of his two great ministers (Cardinal Wolsey and Thomas Cromwell) rather than being manipulated by them, and that he exploited the factions during the final years of his reign rather than being 'captured' by each of them in turn.

However, the 'weak' school remains very active. Its members have judged Henry to have been essentially lacking in confidence, from which they have seen most of his other characteristics stemming. Thus, in their view, he was a ditherer, uncertain of which policy to pursue, suggestible, having no direction of his own to follow; a bully, having enormous power but little except whim to guide him in its use; and cruel, needing to convince himself of his own importance by degrading others. Those who have accepted the essentials of this interpretation have seen Wolsey as a real *alter rex*, (alternative king), deciding on policies that he was able to persuade the king to accept almost at will, and only having to change course on those rare occasions when his nominal master intervened briefly but forcefully. Equally, Thomas Cromwell has been viewed as the king's puppet-master, (although he took a lower profile), persuading Henry to break with Rome in order to secure the end of his marriage to Catherine of Aragon, to dispense with Anne Boleyn when her strong views became tiresome, to plunder the monasteries in order to solve his financial problems, and to institute a reign of terror by which anybody who voiced the least opposition to the royal policy could be charged with treason and executed if need be. Followers of this school have judged the 1540s to have been a time of relative political chaos, with a king who made disastrous decisions as he was buffeted by rival political factions that were led by mediocrities when compared to the ministers of previous decades. Here, it has been thought, lay the origins of the 'Mid-Tudor Crisis'.

3 Henry the King

It is certain that Henry made no distinction between himself as a person and himself as a king. To him they were one and the same thing. He was a 24-hour a day monarch, for he had no private life that existed outside his official capacity. Yet, for him, being king was not a vocation, to be worked at, as it had so obviously been for his father. He regarded it as being a natural state of affairs – as one that required no special effort and no particular training. This was possibly the result of a combination of two factors. He knew from a relatively early age (he was 10 when his elder brother, Arthur, died in 1502) that he was destined to succeed to the throne, and it seems that his father made absolutely no effort to prepare him directly for the responsibilities that were to be his as king. Therefore, he assumed that to be king he merely had to be himself. Hence the importance that historians have attached to their attempts to establish what sort of man Henry was.

This book is not, of course, a biography of Henry. It offers a consideration of one or two strands of national political life during his reign. As a result, Henry is not always 'on stage', and there are large elements of his life that will receive no further consideration in the chapters that follow. After all, Henry devoted only a small amount of time to the activities that are of prime interest to the student of political history. He normally had plenty of (what he considered to be) more important things to do than to deal with the business that historians think of as the affairs of state. If they were lucky, his ministers (or more normally their agents) could persuade the king to turn his mind to the matters that most concerned them for two short periods each day – while he was hearing Mass in the morning and when dinner was over in the evening. But even then he was often reluctant to decide anything and especially to confirm anything with his signature. And there could

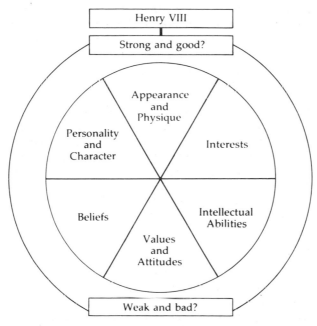

Summary – Henry VIII: The Man and the King

be weeks on end when Henry was totally unprepared to be troubled with such matters. Apart from the rare and relatively brief periods when the king devoted all his considerable energies to government business, Henrician politics were frequently and literally a waiting game.

Despite these provisos, it should be possible for everyone who reads this book to begin to form an opinion about what sort of king Henry VIII was. But any conclusions must, of course, be very provisional. There is much more of the 'story' to be told, and the student of Henry's reign should expect to re-assess his or her opinions about what happened on a regular basis. Fascination there may be, but certainty there will probably never be.

Making notes on 'Henry VIII: the Man and the King'

It is important for you to understand the main arguments and to think about the issues discussed in this chapter, but it is not necessary for you to memorise the detail. You are very unlikely ever to be required to use the material it contains in an examination answer. So, what you write from this chapter is likely to be brief but thoughtful.

Your first task is to identify the issues. The most important is, 'What sort of man and what sort of king was Henry VIII?'. But there are others. They are less important, but they are worth noticing. You will spot them in the first section of the chapter.

Your second task is to define the two 'sides' in the controversy over the main issue.

Your final piece of work is to note down in the form of brief phrases the salient features about Henry as described in sections 2 and 3. The more you think about this the better. The easiest way to do this is to make these notes on a sheet of paper divided into three columns, headed 'strong/good', 'neutral/undecided' and 'weak/bad'. Deciding into which column (or columns) you will write each point will ensure that the most useful thinking is being done.

Source-based questions on 'Henry VIII: The Man and the King'

1 Contemporary descriptions of Henry VIII:
Carefully study the comments made about Henry VIII by contemporaries, given on pages 9, 13 and 15. Answer the following questions.
a) Discuss the opinion that 'Thomas More's sentiments (page 9) were a statement of hope rather than of fact'. (*4 marks*)
b) What is the tone of the comments made on pages 13 and 15? Illustrate your answer with specific examples. (*5 marks*)
c) What are the limitations of the comments quoted as evidence about the young Henry VIII? (*6 marks*)

2 Henry VII and Henry VIII
Study the illustration on page 10. Answer the following questions.
a) Describe the way in which the two kings are portrayed. What evidence is there that the artist intends the viewer to judge Henry VIII the more favourable? (*8 marks*)
b) Given that the drawing was made following Henry VIII's specific instructions to the artist, what conclusions can reliably be drawn from it? (*7 marks*)

CHAPTER 3

England and her Neighbours, 1509–29

1 'Home' and 'abroad'

It might be expected that the phrases 'foreign policy' or 'foreign affairs' would appear in the title of this chapter. After all, this is what it is all about. However, there are some preconceptions that need to be cleared away before such terms can safely be used. Most modern-day thinking about international relations takes place within a framework of assumptions that is not really relevant to the situation in the Europe of the first half of the sixteenth century. To make sense of Henry VIII's dealings with his neighbours it is necessary to make a conscious effort to lay aside the patterns of thought that are used to organise an understanding of modern day foreign affairs.

Some might argue, but not very convincingly, that it may even be necessary to dispense with the very concept of foreign policy when studying events during Henry VIII's reign, as this depends on there being a clear distinction between 'home' and 'abroad'. Where such a distinction was made by the vast majority of Henry VIII's subjects, 'home' was the local area of a few square miles and 'abroad' was everywhere else. There was no identificiation of 'home' with the territories ruled over by the king, or of 'abroad' with other states. This is hardly surprising. Henry VIII's territories in no sense comprised a unitary state. Even the heartland of England, which is the somewhat misleading name with which we label the conglomeration, was not a single entity. Only the south, the east and the midlands were clearly and regularly part of a country centred on London. The inhabitants of the north regarded themselves, and were regarded by southerners, as being largely separate, with different customs, interests and methods of conducting public affairs. The people of the south-west, especially Cornwall, regarded themselves as being virtually independent of England, while most of those living in modern-day Wales thought of the king as a foreign ruler who occasionally interfered in their affairs. This was despite the fact that Wales had been technically incorporated into England in the thirteenth century. Royal influence was particularly weak in the more than 130 virtually independent lordships, collectively known as the Marches, which made up most of eastern Wales and the western fringes of the English midlands.

The territories divided from the mainland by varying amounts of water tended to identify even less with the Henrician state. The largest and richest of these was Ireland, of which Henry was rarely more than nominal lord, even after he assumed the title of King of Ireland in 1541. As long as they did not make too much display of their independence, the nobles of the island were left to run the country much as they wished. Very much smaller, and of insignificance except when invasion threatened, were the Isle of Wight and the Scilly Isles. The Channel Isles fell into a similar category, but as they could not be used as a route into England, they did not assume even temporary significance. This was not the case with Calais, the only other part of the original Norman state that remained in Henry's possession. The port, with its surrounding 'pale' of English territory, was the front line for most of the king's attempts to interfere militarily in the affairs of Europe. It was strategically very well placed and could act as a secure base for offensive action against either France or the Netherlands, and as such was, in Henry's opinion, a valuable asset to be defended at almost any cost.

If 'home' was not a unitary concept to most of Henry's subjects, then 'abroad' was even less coherent. There were a few well known states. Scotland and France were the most obvious of these because they were generally perceived as being 'the enemy'. Northerners were particularly aware of Scotland as a hostile power and as the source of perennially threatened raids, while southerners looked upon France as the country with which their rulers had been at war (with frequent breaks) for several centuries. Conflict with these neighbours was therefore generally regarded as being a 'normal' state of affairs. The Netherlands (or Low Countries) were widely thought of as an area of vital importance, being the supplier of most imports and the recipient of most exports, especially wool and cloth. But there was little awareness of them as a state with a single ruler as opposed to a geographic area with a specific trading function. This was despite the fact that most of the provinces of the Netherlands had long been an integral part of the Burgundian state, which had been inherited by the Austrian Habsburgs, and which, during most of Henry's reign, was one of the cores of Charles V's extensive personal empire.

Outside of this 'inner-ring' of territories were some of the other states of western Europe. The Holy Roman Empire was nebulous to those who lived in it, let alone to those who viewed it from afar. It was to be found in 'Germany' (a much less meaningful label even than England) and was loosely ruled over by the Emperor who, although elected, was traditionally a member of the Habsburg family. Spain was newly emerging in the popular perception as a state as well as a geographical area, following the destruction of the Moorish states in the south of the Iberian Peninsula, and the inheritance of two of the major Christian kingdoms (Aragon and Castile) by Charles of Habsburg (Charles I of Spain and Charles V as Holy Roman Emperor). Only Portugal remained as an alternative independent state in the peninsula. Italy was correctly perceived as being a geographical expression rather than a state. It was variously regarded as the distant centre of wealth and civilisation, as the home of the Pope whose territories covered much of the central portion of the peninsula, and as the arena in which the King of France, the King of Spain and the Emperor carried out their struggle

England and her near Neighbours in the reign of Henry VIII

for dominance over each other. It was also thought of as the home of some of Europe's major trading states (Venice and Genoa), although these impinged less on the public consciousness in England than did the other major European trading force, the Hanseatic League (the Hanse) of north German ports.

Further afield 'abroad' were the barely recognised non-Christian empires which were generally shrouded in mystery. Foremost among these was the empire of the Turk (the Ottoman Empire), thought of as the great threat to Christendom which was likely at any time to break out and to over-run most of southern Europe. Little was known about it other than that it was believed to be peopled by brutal savages who were obviously in league with the devil. Other empires were known to exist further into Asia, but greater distance reduced the sense of their threat. It was also generally understood that the Spanish explorers had established the existence of a new continent to the west of Europe, but, apart from offering an indeterminate future possibility of plunder, little importance was attached to this.

2 National Interests

For writers of modern political history a key concern when making judgements about a government or a ruler's performance in foreign affairs has been the extent to which the country benefited from the policies being followed. Criteria such as 'the strengthening of the country politically or economically' or 'the enhancement of national reputation' have been the ones normally applied. These were what the early academic historians studying the reign of Henry VIII in the second half of the nineteenth century, had in mind when they formed their judgements of English foreign policy in the period 1509–47. It is not surprising that they found Henry VIII to be wanting, for they were judging him by criteria that bore little relation to his own, or his contemporaries', perception of the activity in which he was engaged.

Henry was typical of most early sixteenth century monarchs in being unaware of the concept of foreign policy as a furtherance of national interests. It was not that he chose to reject the idea, in preference for the pursuit of his own selfish ambitions: it was just that it never really occurred to him that there was any real alternative to the assumptions with which he had grown up. He believed that his territories were his 'property' in a not dissimilar way to that in which a large landowner possessed his estates. It was therefore his duty to utilise his possessions so as to maximise his family's prestige, power and wealth in both the short- and the long-terms. Any benefits or harm he did to his subjects in the process were largely coincidental, and only to be taken as a serious matter if they were likely to impinge on him directly, as by causing civil disturbances or by affecting tax yields.

It follows that writers (whether research historians, students, or

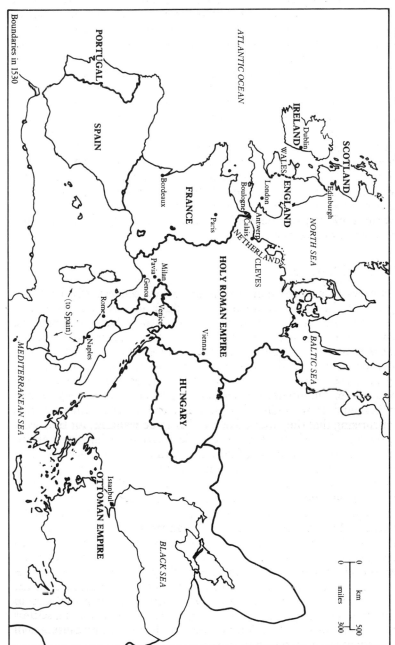

Europe in the reign of Henry VIII

history educators – such as the present author) must be particularly careful to recognise the criteria they are using when they make judgements about Henry VIII's foreign policy. It is widely accepted, although certainly not by everybody, that judgements ought to be made using the criteria that were current at the time of the actions being assessed, and that any judgements made using 'modern standards' should be clearly labelled as what they are (interesting anachronisms?). Perhaps this is why it is important, in advanced historical study, to make a determined effort to understand the context (especially of values and assumptions) in which decisions were made, rather than just finding out 'what happened'.

It is traditional to divide the study of Henry VIII's foreign policy into two parts – 1509–29 and 1529–47. The break-point is the fall of Cardinal Wolsey, who has often been seen as being the real framer of England's foreign policy in the first half of Henry's reign. It is even common usage to talk about 'Wolsey's foreign policy'. This framework for study has advantages, especially in terms of its coherence as an organising idea, but it should be remembered that it is no more than a general approximation to reality. The most obvious shortcomings of this *schema* is that Wolsey did not become even the foremost of the king's advisers – let alone the framer of policy – until 1514, thus leaving the first five years of the reign 'unaccounted for'. A potentially more serious problem is that historians have hotly disputed the extent to which Wolsey ever replaced Henry as the policy maker. All agree that there was effectively a partnership between the two: the dispute is over the relative importance of the partners in setting goals and devising long-term strategies. The evidence does not allow there to be a decisive resolution of the dispute, which will therefore probably continue as long as the period is studied by historians. Although the structure of the discussion that follows implies an acceptance of the traditional view of a period dominated by Wolsey, it should be remembered that there are other equally valid ways of studying the topic.

3 Henry's Early Years

One popular interpretation of events argues that, although Henry was only a young man of 17 when he ascended the throne, he immediately made it clear that he had no intention of living under the shadow of his father's more mature advisers. It is said that his early decision to arrest Empson and Dudley on the charge of high treason because of the methods they had used to extort money for the crown (see page 9), and his early announcement of his intention to marry Catherine of Aragon, after the years of extended delaying tactics employed by Henry VII, signalled his determination to be his own master. It is therefore not surprising that commentators were soon predicting that his aggressive energy would shortly be apparent in his dealings with other rulers.

This likelihood was made almost a certainty by the fact that Henry was an enthusiastic believer in the cause of chivalry (see page 17) and in the concept of the king as a 'valiant knight'. The young Henry saw himself in such a role and he wished to prove his valour by being successful at war. And there was little doubt in people's minds about what that war would be. Henry had been brought up on tales of the heroism of his predecessor, Henry V, who had won famous victories in France, and whose son had been crowned King of France (as well as England). This had resulted in the title of 'King of France' being part of Henry's inheritance from his father. There was every probability that the new King Henry would attempt to make reality match the theory, and that he would mount an expedition across the Channel in an attempt to gain what he claimed was rightly his.

However, even though he was something of a romantic dreamer, Henry was no fool. He could recognise that France had increased greatly in wealth and military strength since England had matched her on the field of battle several generations earlier, and that he would need friends and allies if he were to mount a successful challenge on the European mainland. But he had hopes that such supporters would not be difficult to find. His father-in-law, Ferdinand, was the ruler of the Spanish kingdoms and had been at loggerheads with France for many years because of competing claims to territory both in southern Italy and in the Pyrenees. In addition, the Habsburg family which controlled much of southern Germany and the Burgundian lands (including the Netherlands) (see the map on page 27), as well as holding the title of Holy Roman Emperor, was at odds with France over the possession of Milan, in northern Italy. Henry believed that the creation of an anti-French alliance would be a simple matter.

Yet the new king was to find that 'getting things done' was rather more complicated than he had imagined. He slowly learned that his ministers were not pliant tools in his hands, even when they were given seemingly clear instructions on what they should do. Not only were they skilled in inaction when they did not approve of a policy, but they were also capable of interpreting almost any command in ways that were guaranteed to frustrate their master's intentions. Archbishop Warham and Bishop Fox, in particular, were keen to continue the policies that had been followed during Henry VII's final years, when the aim had been to avoid the expense of war, while selling English neutrality at the highest possible price. They did not approve of the young hot-head whom cruel fate had given them as a king. They were not slow to make their views known to Henry who, at first, did not know how to circumvent them. He was even tricked by them into renewing the truce with France in 1510, when what he really wanted was an excuse to declare war. But he gradually found ways of getting his own way. He learnt that he needed a man of business who would be loyal to him rather than to one of his ministers. He found such a person in Thomas Wolsey, who was supposedly a follower of Bishop Fox.

However, even with a reliable servant to carry out his wishes, Henry did not find it easy to achieve what he desired. He discovered that his potential allies were even less reliable than his reluctant ministers. In particular, he found that Ferdinand of Spain was unscrupulous and totally dishonest, being prepared to break even the most solemn of promises if it appeared to be in his best interests to do so – making the most implausible of excuses after the event. The Emperor Maximilian was little better. As a result, painstaking and costly diplomatic efforts to cement an alliance against France were sabotaged when bribes from the intended victim of the agreement were sufficient to detach England's intended allies one by one. But in 1512 victory seemed to be in sight. Agreement was reached with Ferdinand for a joint attack on France, with England's prize being the acquisition of Aquitaine (the area around Bordeaux), which she had held for much of the middle ages. An English army was therefore sent by sea to northern Spain in readiness for the co-ordinated campaign. But once again Henry was tricked by his father-in-law. While the English army rotted with insufficient supplies and little local support, Ferdinand took advantage of the distraction offered by the presence of an English army so close to the French border to conquer the territory he coveted in the Pyrenees. The remains of Henry's troops made their way home in disgrace at the end of the season having achieved absolutely nothing, but at great expense.

Henry was not slow to learn from the experience. He decided that in the 1513 campaigning season the English army would retain its capability for independent action by operating under his personal command in northern France, within easy reach of Calais. Then, if either of his allies (Ferdinand and Maximilian) failed to do as they had promised, the consequences need not be too disastrous because he would still be able to carry out part of his plan. The task of organising the assemblage of the English army with all necessary supplies, and of ensuring its safe transport across the Channel was entrusted to Wolsey. He performed a near miracle, showing himself to have outstanding energy and administrative ability, and Henry was able to take the field in France with an army that would have been a match for almost any contemporary opposition. But, unfortunately for Henry, the French were too experienced to risk a major encounter with such a force. They knew that the damage it could do was very limited if it was not challenged in a face-to-face encounter. As it could only move a few miles each day – such was the cumbersome nature of its transport – the season would be over before it could reach any target of real significance. So Henry had to satisfy himself with a leisurely progress through the fields of northern France. The minor town of Thérouanne was besieged and taken, only to be given over to Maximilian and his troops to be sacked and burned to the ground. There was still enough time to reach the episcopal city of Tournai (a French enclave within imperial territory) and to force it to surrender after only a token resistance. The citizens feared that stiffer opposition would bring it the same fate as had befallen Thérouanne, and there was no prospect of a relieving force coming to their rescue.

The capture of Tournai was the one significant achievement of the campaign. Although it was a city of no great economic or strategic importance, it was at least a name that was known internationally, and its capture therefore carried some prestige. But there was little real fighting for the English to celebrate. Henry tried to make much of a running skirmish with what was essentially a French observation force that by mistake came too near to the English army. The encounter, which Henry missed because he was not with the army at the time, was officially referred to as a battle (the Battle of the Spurs) in the hope that it would bring some reflected glory to the king. This stratagem was made more credible by the fact that several French noblemen were captured during the 'battle' and could be sent back to England as living proof that a victory had been gained. But historians have generally been scathing about the campaign's achievements on the grounds that it had cost a great amount – more than Henry VII had saved up during twenty years of parsimony – and had inflicted no significant damage on the French. They compare them with the dramatic defeat of the Scots by a second English army in the battle of Flodden which took place while the king was 'wasting his time' in France, and which effectively removed the Scottish menace to England for several decades. However, it should be remembered that it had achieved much of what Henry had intended. He had been seen at the head of an impressive army and he had secured whatever victories were possible. It was very public knowledge that the Emperor had served under his flag and in his pay, and that he had yielded precedence to the King of England in the celebrations following the surrender of Tournai. As far as Henry was concerned, he had matched up to the standards of valour and military leadership that were expected of a king. And there was always the next year.

Henry returned from France in the autumn of 1513 confident that 1514 would see him crowned King of France. But the winter and the spring brought disillusionment. Not only were Maximilian and Ferdinand bribed by the French to disown their treaty obligations to England, but the fact that the royal finances could not support a repetition of the campaign of 1513 was finally accepted by the young warrior. So, instead of overthrowing the King of France, Henry made peace with him. The terms were not ungenerous to England, given the limited room for manoeuvre that Henry enjoyed. In essence, England was bought off by a French promise to make good the arrears in the pension that Henry VII had negotiated for himself and his successors in the 1490s. In addition, Henry was allowed to retain the territory he had seized the previous year. However, in some ways the price paid was high. No English money was involved, but Henry agreed to 'spend' the only currency he possessed for playing the dynastic marriage 'game' that was such an important part of diplomatic activity at the time. His sister Mary was given as wife to Louis XII, the King of France. The fact that she was being betrothed to a toothless old man (he was 52) when she was in love with someone else was greatly distressing for her. But it did not upset Henry, who maintained that she should have known what was to be her role in life. However, he should have been annoyed with himself for sacrificing so valuable an asset for so little potential gain. He must have realised that it would be many years, at best, before he would have another near relative to offer in the international marriage market.

4 Wolsey in Control

By the time that peace was signed with France, Henry had lost much of his interest in day-to-day diplomacy. He had become very impatient with the hard work that it involved. He was still keen to win glory, but he was content for someone else to arrange it for him. This someone was Thomas Wolsey. But Wolsey, despite his brilliance, was relatively inexperienced in the intricacies of international relations, and was initially no match for the established experts in the craft, such as the Emperor Maximilian. It was not that Wolsey made elementary mistakes – he generally did not – but rather that the continuing pursuit of a 'forward' policy, as demanded by Henry, constantly left him vulnerable to the trickery of others. Wolsey was well aware that the agreement made with France in 1514 was to be regarded as no more than a lull in the struggle between two ancient enemies. He also recognised that financial considerations dictated that his strategy must be to fund others to attack France, which could be done more cheaply, once again, than putting an English army into the field on the continent. The problem was that those who were most readily available to be used in this way (the Emperor Maximilian and the Swiss) were also the most skilled at receiving money and then doing as little as possible to earn it. Thus, by the end of the 1517 campaigning season, considerable further English expenditure had only resulted in inconclusive campaigns that had done nothing to weaken the French position.

In the meantime, the personalities on the international scene had changed considerably. Louis XII had died within a few months of marrying Mary (no causal relationship has been suggested) and had been succeeded by his nephew, Francis I. Francis was as talented and ambitious as his English counterpart, and his accession was taken as a personal challenge by Henry, who was determined not to be bettered by his younger rival. The rivalry was intense from the outset (January 1515) as Francis immediately pulled off a very public prestige *coup*. He aided and abetted Henry's best friend, the Duke of Suffolk, in marrying Mary (the Dowager Queen of France) when he visited the French court to accompany her back to England. Francis pretended that he did this merely to smooth the course of true love, because Mary and Suffolk had been secretly promised to each other before they had been separated by the terms of the peace treaty of 1514, but everybody knew that his real motive was to cause Henry a loss of face. For not only had the King of England's sister entered a second marriage without permission, which would normally be regarded as treason, but she had also taken as husband the man whom her brother had trusted most completely. Thus the insult could hardly have been greater. In addition, Henry had been robbed of a second chance to use his sister in the dynastic marriage market, thus weakening his international bargaining position. It is not surprising that Henry's fury was difficult to keep within bounds. Although Wolsey's subsequent claim that only his spirited intercession saved Suffolk's life has been doubted by historians because it is uncorroborated, it has the ring of authenticity about it. Francis could hardly have found a more wounding way of announcing to the world that Henry was not to be the uncontested leader of the younger generation of European rulers. It is little wonder that for some time Henry routinely sought from visitors to his court the assurance that he outshone Francis in all respects – from the shapeliness of his calf to the splendour of his entertainments! Thus a deep-seated national rivalry was heightened by an intense personal rivalry between two young kings.

A third young and powerful ruler made his entrance on the international scene when Ferdinand of Spain died in 1516. He was the 15-year-old Charles of Habsburg, who by succeeding Ferdinand added the Spanish kingdoms to his existing Burgundian lands (see the map on page 27). As he was also the heir to the Emperor Maximilian, who was generally believed to be near the end of his life, the prospect was that Charles would soon rule over the largest personal empire that had existed in Europe for many centuries. Henry was painfully aware that both Francis and Charles would have resources at their disposal that were beyond his own wildest dreams. It was therefore unlikely that he would be able to challenge them successfully in battle. As a consequence, he would have to seek the international glory for which he yearned in ways other than through warfare. It is likely that the suggestion that he seek to enhance his reputation by becoming the peacemaker of Europe came from Wolsey, who by 1517 had grown sufficiently in confidence to attempt to formulate policies of his own.

5 Wolsey's Foreign Policy

For much of the last century and a half during which researchers have been studying the history of early Tudor England, it has been assumed that the foreign policy of the 15 years following 1514 was Wolsey's.

Accounts have been written almost as if, during these years, Henry VIII only existed to rubber stamp the decisions made by his minister. However, this view has been challenged in recent decades as the interplay between the two men has been more clearly revealed by further research. But no definitive picture has so far emerged. While it is apparent that Wolsey made most decisions on a day-to-day basis and occasionally took major initiatives without the prior agreement, or even knowledge, of his master, it is equally certain that Henry intervened decisively at times to redirect events as he wished them to go. Additional complications are presented by the fact that, in order to maintain the confidence of the king, Wolsey had at least to appear to be implementing Henry's policies, even if he was in practice pursuing objectives of his own. Given the partial nature of the surviving evidence – many of the important exchanges between Henry and Wolsey were by word of mouth, either direct or via a trusted third party – and the fact that much of the extant documentary evidence is in the form of letters that were originally written to deceive, and are therefore unreliable as pointers to aims or motives, it is not surprising that it can not be established beyond reasonable doubt whether Wolsey was manipulating Henry, or whether he was essentially carrying out the king's wishes. The most that can safely be maintained is that Henry played a more significant role in the formulation and conduct of 'Wolsey's foreign policy' than has traditionally been allowed.

It has been customary for writers on Wolsey's foreign policy to present an analysis that revolves around the consistent pursuit of a coherent aim or strategy. Up to the time of the First World War the orthodox interpretation was that Wolsey sought to 'maintain the balance of power', which, surprisingly enough, was the way in which contemporary British foreign policy was viewed at the time! It was argued that this aim was pursued in order to preserve some say for England in foreign affairs by ensuring that no one person (Charles or Francis) attained such dominance that he could arrange matters without taking into account the interests of other states, such as England. The claim was that Wolsey followed this policy by threatening to give his support to whichever side seemed likely to be worsted by the other. It was maintained that this policy was generally successful in ensuring that England's international status remained high.

This interpretation became discredited when Pollard, writing in the 1920s, established a new orthodoxy that was to survive for 40 years. His contention was that Wolsey was a slavish follower of papal policy, changing England's stance whenever he was asked to do so by the Pope. His motives were said to be a mixture of principle and self-interest. It was claimed that, as the Pope's representative in England, Wolsey believed that it was his duty to do as his spiritual master directed, even at the expense of frustrating the wishes of his king, and that he had a vested interest in doing so because he aspired to be elected Pope at some stage. In the 1960s Scarisbrick demolished this interpretation by showing that Wolsey ignored papal instructions as frequently as he followed them and by casting serious doubt on the genuineness of Wolsey's ambition to become Pope. He argued that Wolsey's support of papal diplomatic initiatives was largely coincidental and happened merely because both England and the Papacy shared common interests from time to time. Scarisbrick went on to establish a new orthodoxy based on the existence of a main aim and of a preferred method. The aim was the establishment and maintenance of peace. The method was a variant of the old 'balance of power' interpretation. This he established by turning the old argument on its head and claiming that Wolsey sought to achieve an 'unbalance of power' – that he tried always to join the stronger side so that it would create a sufficient imbalance for the other side to realise that fighting was pointless. He claimed that this policy has not been more apparent to observers because Wolsey was not very good at implementing it and frequently made mistakes which he attempted to justify by pretending that his aims and methods were other than they had been.

In many ways it is a healthy sign that the Scarisbrick interpretation has not been replaced by an alternative single-faceted explanation. This is perhaps because it has become more and more apparent that no coherent pattern ever existed in Wolsey's approach to diplomacy. It is now widely accepted that although there were threads that ran through numbers of incidents, there was no single guiding principle that directed his actions throughout his 15 years in power. At differing times he was motivated by selfish considerations – especially a desire to obtain more extensive or longer lasting delegated powers from the Pope – by the need to satisfy the expectations of Henry VIII, by a wish to further what he considered to be national or papal interests, and by an altrustic inclination to benefit mankind by inaugurating an era of peace. It is possible to detect many or all of these motives in each of the decisions he made, but the evidence is not full enough for it to be possible to comment on the relative importance of these motives in any but highly speculative terms.

6 Wolsey the Peace Maker

In October 1518 the Treaty of London was inaugurated, with England and France as the first signatories. Within a few months it had been adhered to by many other states, including Spain and the Papacy. At the time it was thought to be a triumph for Wolsey and to have reflected considerable glory on Henry VIII. It was truly a 'grandiose scheme', intended to bind the 20 leading states of Europe to perpetual peace with one another. The plan was for all those states with an active foreign policy not only to commit themselves to non-aggression but to promise to make war on any ruler who contravened the treaty, thus making it impossible for any state to benefit from attacking another. The publicly quoted aspiration was for the treaty to bring an end to warfare between the Christian states of Europe.

Historians have generally viewed this initiative as yet another example of Wolsey's cynical self-seeking. There is much evidence to support this interpretation. Although there is incontrovertible documentary evidence that he had been working on his grand design before the Pope took a similar initiative – the papal plan was for a five year truce between the powers during which a crusade against the Turks would take place – the public perception was that Wolsey was working to implement the Pope's wishes. It was important to Wolsey that this should be so because he was using the fact that he was acting as the Pope's representative to win for himself the status of *legatus a latere* (see page 49) that he so much desired. It has even been claimed that this was his primary motivation in the affair. Others have maintained that he was merely seeking to satisfy his sense of his own importance by being seen to be the peacemaker of Europe, and to be treated as such during the extensive public celebrations that accompanied the unveiling of the treaty. Few have been prepared to admit that there may have been a serious intention behind Wolsey's actions. But if there was not, he was guilty of sacrificing national interests for personal gain, for the price paid for French adherence to the treaty was the return of Tournai (admittedly at a very fair price) and the promise (easily revoked) that Mary, at the time Henry's only surviving child, would be married to the King of France's eldest son in due course.

Over the next two years Wolsey worked to build on the foundations that had been laid by the Treaty of London. His efforts were generously rewarded in 1520 when Henry and Francis met at the Field of Cloth of Gold, near to the border between the two monarchs' possessions outside Calais. The meeting was one of the most spectacular events in modern European history. It lasted for a fortnight and was participated in by a large portion of the senior ruling élites of the two countries. In fact, the representation was so complete (about 3000 from each side) that very few people of national importance were left behind in England to manage affairs during their colleagues' absence. The two kings vied strenuously with each other in order to create as splendid an impression as possible. No expense was spared in providing the most sumptuous of feasts ('a gastronomic marathon') and entertainments (with daily jousting meticulously carried out according to the medieval rules of chivalry still accepted in both countries at the time), the most richly decorated costumes for the participants, and the most elaborate of settings. The French prepared a village of richly decorated tents and pavilions to accommodate their party. Its cost was enormous – roughly equivalent to one year of Henry VIII's normal income – and its preparation was a triumph of planning and organisation. Western Europe had to be scoured to locate the huge quantities of luxury materials required. For example, the accounts showed that 72,544 *fleur de lis* of gold thread mounted on blue velvet were purchased to decorate the walls of the royal pavilions. Unfortunately, much of the effort was wasted as high winds and heavy rain meant that most of the erections had to be dismantled within a few days of their completion. The English effort was much more successful. Its centrepiece was a temporary palace to accommodate the king and a handful of his leading courtiers – the rest of the party lodged in discomfort in a 'settlement' of about 800 tents. The palace was considered to be one of the wonders of the age, such was the splendour of its design and decoration (see the illustration on page 38), and it drew sightseers from far and wide. This was partly, no doubt, because of the two fountains at its entrance which constantly dispensed free wine to all and sundry. The total edifice had taken many hundreds of workmen several months to construct.

1 So great resort thither came, that both knights and ladies that were come to see the nobleness were fayn to lie in hay and straw, and held them thereof highly pleased.

However, it seems that the meeting achieved nothing of lasting significance. If it was intended to cement Anglo-French amity it patently failed. The members of the English party whose views are known all seem to have been confirmed in their anti-French prejudices rather than having had them removed or weakened. And no agreements of any importance were reached during the fortnight's celebrations. In fact, it seems that Henry and Francis viewed the occasion as no more than an opportunity to impress others of their wealth and international standing. Certainly the Field of Cloth of Gold did nothing to advance the cause of general peace. If anything, it created problems for Wolsey in convincing the rest of Europe that England was not taking sides in the already developing struggle for supremacy between Francis I and Charles V. Meetings between Henry and Charles were arranged to take place both before and after the Field of Cloth of Gold so that the clear message could be given that there was no English partiality towards France. The fact that these meetings were necessary substantiates the view that the extravaganza in France was essentially a public relations exercise, rather than being a contribution to the cause of general European peace. It is significant that Henry was most grateful to Wolsey for making it appear to the world that he was the equal of the two 'super power' rulers of Europe (no mention of peace making), and that the events of 1520 further confirmed Wolsey in the favour of his monarch. It is impossible to establish the extent to which this factor loomed large in Wolsey's thinking.

The palace and fountains from 'The Field of Cloth of Gold'

7 Wolsey and the Papal Tiara

Pollard's contention that Wolsey seriously aspired to be elected to the papal throne was based on considerable evidence. It is certain that at times during the electoral processes following the deaths of Leo X in 1521 and of his successor, Adrian VI, in 1523, Wolsey confidently expected to be the successful candidate. He had good reason for his optimism. Not only had Charles V promised to lend his weight to Wolsey's cause, but the news from Rome was of a large amount of positive support among the electoral body of cardinals. But, in the event, it transpired that Wolsey had been misled. In the first election Charles actually pressed for an alternative candidate (his ex-tutor, who was actually elected), and in the second election he purposely failed to make his wishes known in time. What is more, the cardinals who had appeared to be so strongly in Wolsey's support, turned out to have been doing no more than angling for financial inducements. Thus there was never any realistic possibility that Wolsey would be chosen as Pope.

It now appears that Wolsey generally accepted that this was the case, and only made genuine attempts to secure his own election during the moments when the evidence available to him suggested that he was wrong and that his prospects really were good. For the rest of the time he was probably only humouring those who wished to advance his cause. Evidence that was unknown to Pollard suggests that the initial proposal for Wolsey's candidature came from Charles V, who was probably attempting to create in Henry VIII a 'want' that he would then be able to help satisfy in return for some other favour. Certainly he was not slow to point out to Henry that his international reputation would be greatly enhanced if his chief minister were to be elected Pope, and Henry seems to have taken the bait because it was often only to satisfy him that Wolsey went through the motions of advancing his own candidature. Although it can never be known for certain, it seems very likely that Wolsey rarely made serious attempts to forward his own papal cause. The major evidence to support this view is provided by a consideration of his long-term dealings with the Papacy. If his aim was to persuade cardinals to vote for him in a future election, he went about it in an untypically ineffectual manner. On numerous occasions he gratuitously insulted the Pope and his advisers, either by failing to answer urgent communications from them, or by constructing replies that were intended to 'score points' rather than to win friends. Wolsey was a skilled politician who would not have made such basic mistakes had his aim been as Pollard claimed.

One strand of Pollard's argument was the evidence of Wolsey's attempts to win support during the electoral periods. He backed this up with a general contention that the thread running through Wolsey's actions in foreign affairs was his desire to curry favour in Rome. This interpretation has long been discredited by later research that has shown both that some of Pollard's conclusions were inaccurate even based on the evidence he used, and that other evidence proves that Wolsey acted in opposition to papal policy almost as often as he supported it. It can now be safely concluded that Wolsey had no long-term aim of becoming Pope, and that his short-term enthusiasms for wearing the papal tiara were flights of fancy based on inaccurate information, and were rapidly jettisoned once the reality of the situation became known to him.

8 Wolsey and the Habsburg-Valois Conflict

When Charles was elected Holy Roman Emperor in 1519 he added the Emperor's quarrel with the Kings of France over Milan to his existing inheritance of Franco-Burgundian and Franco-Spanish rivalries. Therefore, especially given the aggressive personality of Francis I, it was almost inevitable that a simmering Habsburg-Valois conflict would provide the backcloth to western European international relations for the following decades (in fact until 1559). This situation presented Henry VIII and Wolsey with both continuous opportunities and frequent challenges. Given the strategic position that England enjoyed, being able either to disrupt Charles's communications between Spain and the Netherlands or to open a new front in any attack on France, her favours were certain to be in great demand from the two major powers.

It was not long before Wolsey was called on to pay some of the price for his triumph of the Treaty of London. Francis I had been happy enough to receive his reward for agreeing to join the Cardinal's 'grand design' but he had no intention of being constrained by its terms or conditions. He was determined to strengthen his position in northern Italy by military action against Charles and his supporters, and he did not expect the arrangements made in the Treaty of London to be invoked against him. After all, it would be in none of the non-belligerents' interests to do so. As expected, however, Charles called upon England and others to come to his assistance to halt the aggressor. In August 1521 Wolsey travelled in great pomp to Bruges in the Netherlands in order to treat with Charles on the action to be taken. Once again, promises of future support were easily made, especially as it was hoped that a change in the situation would make it unnecessary to fulfil any obligations. The agreement made with Charles was that an English army would invade France unless Francis agreed to make peace. It has frequently been claimed that Wolsey's expectation was that the mere threat of English action would be sufficient to persuade France to make terms. However, it is unlikely that Wolsey was so naïve. He had so much experience of Francis's pig-headedness that he must have realised that a threat was likely to be insufficient. It is much more probable that he gambled on the war being resolved one way or the other before he ran out of delaying tactics for English action. In the meantime, he was more than satisfied with the kudos that his meeting with Charles had brought him.

In the event, Wolsey was unable to prevent the Emperor's friends from persuading Henry VIII that England must take some military action once Francis chose to ignore the warnings he had been given. But he was not as unhappy with the situation as he might have been, because it seemed that a dramatic defeat of the French was in prospect. Charles had managed to secure the support of the Duke of Bourbon, one of the foremost French magnates, who was so discontented with the way in which he had been treated by Francis that he was prepared to risk all in an act of open treachery. It was thought that he would be able to carry a significant portion of the French nobility into rebellion with him. So, although half of the campaigning season was already over, an English army was sent to France at short notice in August 1523. But as so often happened in the sixteenth century, military action proved to be much less decisive than its authors had expected. Bourbon turned out to be a complete disappointment. He only managed to generate minimal support for his cause within France and he soon became, in effect, an armed exile, who despite English money and imperial patronage, was unable to establish himself as a significant factor in the conflict. Thus, even if the English prong of the triple thrust on Paris had not become bogged down in the mud of winter, the allied plan to co-ordinate their forces in a knockout blow on the French capital would have been hamstrung by the failure of Bourbon's army to play its part. As a result, Wolsey's and Henry's passing enthusiasm for armed intervention evaporated, and Wolsey was allowed to implement his orginal strategy of stalling Charles's demands for action while he secretly attempted to negotiate a general peace with the French.

But luck did not favour Wolsey. In February 1525 Charles secured the decisive victory that Wolsey had estimated to be so unlikely. In a battle that took place outside the walls of Pavia, in northern Italy, the unthinkable happened. Not only was the French army totally destroyed as an effective fighting force, but Francis I and most of his leading supporters were captured. This placed Charles in an overwhelmingly dominant position. Henry VIII was not slow to seek advantage of the situation. He realised that here was a rare opportunity to fulfil his intermittently held dream of securing the French crown for himself. A proposal was rapidly prepared for submission to the Emperor whereby France would be dismembered, with Charles and Bourbon receiving the parts to which they could reasonably lay claim, and Henry taking the remainder along with the title of King of France. But little except wishful thinking could have been behind this plan. Although Henry promised to fight alongside him in future as his faithful ally, there was little to commend the proposal to Charles. There was nothing that Henry could really do to hurt him, so there was no need to buy his support by allowing him any of his demands. Certainly there was no point in exchanging one powerful and ambitious King of France for another, and one who controlled extensive territories on both sides of the Channel. Charles judged that the greatest advantage was to be gained by leaving France chastened but not too aggrieved, and therefore not feeling compelled to seek a swift revenge. But sound as this strategy was, it was impossible to implement. Although Francis was forced to swear the most binding of oaths concerning his future conduct, and had to provide his own sons as hostages against his further misbehaviour, he was prepared to launch fresh attacks on Charles within a year of his release. In the meantime he had been freed from his oaths by the Pope on the grounds that they had been extorted under duress, and he had correctly guessed that Charles would not be prepared to risk international odium by harming his hostages.

At first Henry and Wolsey could do little but rage impotently. Henry did have hopes of launching an attack on France while she was leaderless, but he was forced to abandon these when he was unable to raise the necessary finance. It has been suggested that Wolsey was less than enthusiastic about this venture, as shown by his lack of determination in making a success of the nationwide 'Amicable Grant' of 1525 which was to have provided the money for it. But the evidence is by no means conclusive. However, Wolsey was certainly diligent in encouraging the formation of an anti-imperial alliance (the League of Cognac) in northern Italy in 1526, with which France could associate in her efforts to reverse the verdict of Pavia. He was also prepared to sign an alliance with France the next year threatening Charles with English intervention if he did not make a satisfactory peace with his opponents. This resulted in an English declaration of war on Charles in 1528, but it was little more than a gesture. No English army was put into the field and a separate agreement was made to ensure that London's trade with the Netherlands was not interrupted. It was therefore not surprising that England was only included at the last minute in the Treaty of Cambrai, negotiated between Francis and Charles in 1529 to bring the fighting to an end. If Wolsey had not engineered an English presence in the final stages of the negotiations, it would have been even clearer than it already was that Henry VIII was no longer being treated as an equal by the King of France and the Holy Roman Emperor. Thus Wolsey's final piece of major diplomacy before his fall in October 1529 was no more than a face-saving exercise for an increasingly unappreciative master.

9 Assessment

Most historians have been highly critical of Henry VIII's and Wolsey's foreign policies in the period 1509 to 1529. But there has been little consistency in the nature of these criticisms. England's dealings with her neighbours during these years have been variously described as mis-directed, muddled, costly failures, naïve, and shameful. Although some of these judgements tell us more about the values and assumptions of those who made them than they do about the issue under consideration, there is no escaping the fact that whatever criteria for assessment have been chosen the resulting conclusions have rarely been complimetary to either the king or his leading minister.

The least controversial sets of criteria for judgement used by historians tend to be those which concentrate on the extent to which a person managed to achieve his or her aims and objectives. However, it is rare for any writer carrying out an assessment to be satisfied with such a limited range of criteria. It is very normal for the aims and objectives themselves to be held up for scrutiny, and for comment to be made on their appropriateness as well as on their practicality. It is, of course, the issue of appropriateness that gives rise to most subjectivity on the part of commentators. As objectivity has been at the centre of the code of professionalism aspired to by British historians in the twentieth century, this has generally been frowned upon by most of those who have researched English history during the last 100 years. But it must be remembered that in many societies the concept of objective history is anathema, and that any account of the past that does not reflect the prevailing value system is highly suspect. However, all students of history in a 'free' society are likely to be encouraged to construct their own set of criteria for making judgements about the past, and will probably be rightly suspicious of those handed down to them by others.

Thus the first task in making an assessment of England's foreign relations during the first half of Henry VIII's reign is to identify the criteria to be used. It seems safe to assume that most people will wish to include 'degree of success' in their assessment, and that this will be measured against Henry's and Wolsey's aspirations. If this is the case, there is probably room for a less critical conclusion to be reached than has often been drawn in the past. Although there were some obvious large-scale failures, especially between 1525 and 1529, there were many occasions on which both Henry and Wolsey had good reason to think that they had been very successful. After the campaign of 1513 Henry knew that he was internationally regarded as a figure of splendid chivalric kingship and his certainty was increased by events such as those at the Field of Cloth of Gold in 1520. Wolsey was equally successful in creating an outstanding reputation and status for himself (especially in being made *legatus a latere* for life in 1524) which meant that he was treated as being virtually on a par with the leading rulers of Europe. These were no mean achievements to set against the periodic frustrations that beset both men's diplomatic ventures and which became increasingly frequent in the latter stages of their partnership.

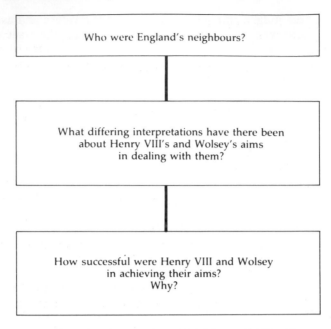

Summary – England and her Neighbours, 1509–29

Making notes on 'England and her Neighbours, 1509–29'

This is the first chapter of the book on which you should be encouraged to make detailed notes, as it covers issues that comprise both an important examination topic in its own right and form a vital component of any overall consideration of the career of Thomas Wolsey, for which the next chapter is also essential.

As you make your notes be consciously attempting i) to identify Henry's and Wolsey's aims in foreign affairs, and, ii) to judge the extent of their success. Thus you will be writing about 'issues' rather than just recording 'facts'.

You may find that the following headings and questions will form a helpful framework for your notes.

1. Home and Abroad
2. National interests
   For these sections it might be worth concentrating on the question 'What modern assumptions need to be questioned when studying the international relations of the early sixteenth century?'
3. Henry's Early Years

3.1. What did Henry wish to achieve?

3.2. How far was he successful in achieving his goals?

4. Wolsey's control
   In what ways did the context of England's foreign policy change between 1514 and 1517?

5. Wolsey's foreign policy
   Identify the changing general interpretations of Wolsey's foreign policy.

6. Wolsey the Peace Maker

6.1. The Treaty of London

6.2. The Field of Cloth of Gold

7. Wolsey and the Papal Tiara
   What was Wolsey's attitude towards the possibility of him becoming Pope?

8. Wolsey and the Habsburg-Valois conflict
   Why was Wolsey generally unsuccessful in foreign affairs between 1525 and 1529?

9. Assessment
   Make an assessment of the success of Wolsey's foreign policy using criteria of your own choosing. Clearly state what these criteria are.

Source-based questions on'England and her Neighbours, 1509–29'

1 The Field of Cloth of Gold, 1520
Carefully study the illustration of the English palace at the Field of Cloth of Gold (page 38) and read the contemporary description of visitors to the palace (page 37). Answer the following questions.

a) Using evidence from both the illustration and the extract identify the type of people who were allowed to visit the English palace. Why was this so? (*3 marks*)

b) Contemporaries were impressed by the size of the windows in the palace. Why would this have been so? What else about it might they have been impressed by? (*5 marks*)

c) What were the likely motives of Henry VIII in spending so much money on a building that was to be demolished after a fortnight? (*4 marks*)

d) What was the historical significance of the Field of Cloth of Gold? (*3 marks*)

CHAPTER 4

Cardinal Wolsey

The career of Cardinal Wolsey was one of the most amazing episodes in an amazing reign. Thomas Wolsey was born the son of a butcher in Ipswich in 1472 or 1473. From these lowly origins he defied all the rules of social mobility by becoming the richest and most powerful man in England besides the king. It has often been claimed that he acted as the effective ruler of the country (as an *alter rex*) for the 15 years up to his fall in 1529. At the height of his influence, in the mid-1520s, his word was almost law and it was widely understood both at home and abroad that there was little point in attempting to secure any royal favour except through him. His court rivalled the king's in size and splendour and often outstripped it in day-to-day political importance. His palaces, especially Hampton Court and York House (later known as the Palace of Westminster), were developed to be fit for a king, as Henry VIII discovered long before he acquired them for himself. No other commoner was to rival his career for several centuries, and the extent to which he achieved personal political success was unique in Tudor England.

Yet professional historians have generally shunned him. Only one major biography in English has been published, and that appeared in 1929. Peter Gwyn's huge volume which was published in 1990 was essentially a long-term 'labour of love'. Why has Wolsey been so ignored? It is certainly not because there is a lack of available documentary evidence about his activities. If anything, there is almost too much, although on any one issue there is rarely enough detail for an uncontestable conclusion to be drawn. Because he operated in the arena of international political and church affairs, as well as within all aspects of English public life, there is a mass of relevant research material scattered throughout the archives of Europe. It would take a full lifetime of study to become familiar with it all. But it is probably not the daunting nature of the task that explains historians' reluctance systematically to up-date Pollard's pioneering biography which was researched so long ago, in the years immediately before and after the First World War. It is more that Wolsey is widely viewed as being a historical dead-end; the last of a long line of powerful medieval royal servants who was almost an anachronism in his own time, and therefore not a very worthwhile subject of study. He is seen as being the end of something rather than being the beginning; as someone who had little long-term effect on anything, and therefore as being of little historical significance. In these circumstances there has seemed little justification for devoting a professional career to studying his activities. To do so might almost seem to be self-indulgent antiquarianism. But, of course,

not everybody would accept the prevailing orthodoxy on the justifica-
tions for undertaking historical research.

1 Rise to Pre-eminence

How was it that the low-born butcher's son was able to become the
'better' of the entire English aristocracy?

It would be surprising if it were not because of a mixture of merit and
good fortune. Wolsey was outstandingly able. He possessed a very fine
mind which was apparent from very early in his life. He took
considerable pleasure in recounting in later years how he had been sent
to Oxford as a relatively young boy, and had been awarded the
unofficial title of boy-bachelor because he had gained his first degree at
the age of 15. But it was his character and personality that marked him
out as much more than a young man of high intellectual ability. He
possessed the drive and confidence necessary to seize the opportunities
that came his way. He was seemingly afraid of nothing (certainly not of
failure) and he was prepared to take calculated risks whenever the need
arose. One contemporary reported (although some historians doubt the
reliability of the account) that when he was put in charge of his college
funds he made the unilateral decision to initiate some ambitious
building works, assuming that his colleagues would be too timid to
challenge his authority. He was wrong, and had rapidly to seek
preferment elsewhere. But it was in winning the patronage of important
people that he showed the essential attributes of the up-and-coming
man. He could flatter obsequiously while at the same time making
himself welcome as an interesting and attractive companion. And most
importantly, he could be relied upon to carry out whatever task was
entrusted to him with exemplary skill and application. He thrived on
hard and intensive work in an age when most people sought and found a
gentle pace of life. This marked him out from most of his potential
competitors, as did his single-minded and totally unscrupulous pursuit
of his objectives. If anybody got in his way they were elbowed aside
with whatever force was necessary. Many tales exist about his nefarious
activities as a young man. It does not matter that many of them are
probably apocryphal. What is significant is that Wolsey liked to pretend
that they were true, presumably because they showed him as the type of
person (an unprincipled and selfish go-getter) he was pleased to be.

He first came to major notice during the final years of Henry VII's
reign as the man of business for Bishop Fox. Fox was one of the king's
more trusted counsellors, and Wolsey was able to shine as a most
efficient and flamboyant conductor of the king's business. However, his
major break came in the situation that prevailed in the early years of the
new king's reign. Henry VIII was initially surrounded by most of his
father's old counsellors. This is not to be wondered at because he came
to the throne at the age of 17, having lived a life virtually devoid of

public business, and having no followers of his own to promote to senior positions. However, what angered Henry and gave Wolsey his chance was that the old counsellors seemed very reluctant to become the new king's men. They not only tried to brow-beat him into continuing his father's policies (especially in foreign affairs) when what he wanted was to follow a 'forward' policy of his own, but they also constantly criticised him for not taking his kingly 'work' duties seriously enough, and for spending too much time in leisure pursuits, such as hunting and feasting. Wolsey later claimed that he took advantage of the situation by giving the king the advice he wanted to hear, thus winning his approbation. At the same time he claimed to have encouraged the king to continue with his life of gaiety while leaving the boring work of government to people such as him, who could be relied on to carry out the king's wishes, which the senior counsellors could not be trusted to do. Although it has rightly been pointed out that Wolsey oversimplified matters in his reported account of events, it is highly likely that his version accurately reflected the spirit of what happened. It is just that it foreshortened events, making it seem that what took several years was achieved in one shrewd move.

Wolsey was also assisted by the fact that many of the leading figures from the previous reign were either removed from the scene, such as Empson and Dudley, or were pleased to seek a quieter life in political retirement, such as Archbishop Warham and Bishop Fox. This left Wolsey a relatively uncontested route in his rise to the top. But he still had to prove himself worthy of the king's confidence. His opportunity to do this in a resounding manner came in 1512–13. Somebody was needed to organise the expeditionary force to invade France under Henry's leadership in the summer of 1513. Wolsey was prepared to take on this responsibility, despite the fact that more senior and experienced officials shrank from a challenge that was likely to bring nothing but problems and aggravation, followed by criticism over what was almost certain to be a disaster. But Wolsey defied all the pundits by achieving the seemingly impossible. He ensured that all the right people and supplies were in the right places at the right times. In the process he antagonised most of those in authority by riding roughshod over their rights and sensibilities in order to achieve results in the necessary timescales, arguing at every turn that the king's wishes must take precedence over all other considerations. However, the more people complained to Henry about Wolsey's ruthlessness in getting done what was necessary, the more the king warmed to the servant who seemed able to overcome all obstacles in implementing his wishes. By the middle of 1514 Henry was referring almost all matters of business to Wolsey, in the certainty that they would be dealt with efficiently, and generally along the lines that he desired.

 * In the circumstances Henry was not well placed to resist whatever

See Preface for explanation of * symbol.

requests Wolsey might make of him for his own advancement, given that his informal position as the king's chief minister was not reflected in any official appointments. Wolsey was not slow to utilise the argument that the king's honour and dignity demanded that his leading counsellor should both hold positions of the greatest possible status and receive an income that allowed him to adopt a lifestyle befitting his standing as Henry's most favoured servant. The cheapest way for Henry to reward Wolsey was by securing his appointment to posts that were funded other than from the royal finances. The Church was traditionally the source of such preferments. Before his emergence as a leading counsellor, Wolsey had already benefited from appointment to posts of secondary importance within the Church, such as being made Dean of Lincoln. Once the success of 1513 was behind him, he was in line for major appointments. In rapid succession he was made Bishop of Tournai (particularly fitting for the man who had made its capture by Henry possible, although he was never able to make good his claim to this position), Bishop of Lincoln, and Archbishop of York. The Archbishopric was particularly significant because it made Wolsey the second most senior person within the Church in England.

However, Wolsey was rarely satisfied with second best. He wished to be seen to be number one. Although the leading position within the English Church (the Archbishopric of Canterbury) was held by a man who made it very clear that he had no intention of resigning in order to make way for the king's favourite, there was another way of securing clerical pre-eminence for Wolsey. The Pope could appoint him to a position that outranked Canterbury. A campaign to exert pressure on the Pope to do so was orchestrated by Wolsey and was fully supported by Henry. In 1515 Leo X succumbed to the pressure and made Wolsey a cardinal, a position that outranked all churchmen except the Pope. But this did not satisfy the new 'prince of the Church' because, although it gave him precedence over Archbishop Warham of Canterbury on ceremonial occasions, it did not give him control over the English Church as a whole. This remained in Warham's hands, and to reverse the situation a further honour would be necessary. Wolsey would have to be appointed the highest category of papal representative, a *legatus a latere* – a position normally awarded for a specific purpose so that a representative with full papal powers could be present at a decision-making occasion far distant from Rome. Wolsey, with Henry's assistance, campaigned vigorously to receive such an appointment. In 1518 he engineered a situation whereby he was accorded the honour, along with a fellow cardinal sent from Rome, to act on the Pope's behalf in negotiations for what was hoped to become a general truce between the major European states. This was to be done so that a crusade against the Turks could take place. By exploiting every diplomatic advantage he could, Wolsey at first secured the extension of his legatine powers for a number of years, and then in 1524 contrived to win what for him was the major prize – the confirmation of his powers for life. This was a remarkable achievement and was for Wolsey the most cherished of his positions.

There was much less need for Wolsey to be appointed to official positions within the state than there was for formal grants of power within the Church. After all, he enjoyed the full support of the head of state (Henry VIII), whereas he was never in a similar position with the Pope in Rome. As long as the king was prepared to back him up in his decisions, Wolsey had nothing to fear from his fellow countrymen. In the early sixteenth century the government was still the king's government in practice as well as in theory, and it was generally accepted that the monarch could change the rules (but not the laws) as and when he wanted. If the king wished to entrust sweeping powers to Wolsey that was his decision and few would contest it, even though existing areas of responsibility were invaded in the process. The way the system worked in practice had been well illustrated at the time when Wolsey was organising the expedition to France in 1513. Although he had held none of the major offices of state he had been able to mobilise the whole machinery of government to carry out his commands. This had been possible because the king had willed it. But Wolsey was very concerned about issues of status and precedence. He was not satisfied with the reality of power: he also wished to be seen to be wielding it. He was therefore insistent that Henry should appoint him to the senior office of state, the lord chancellorship. But as was normal in most public affairs at the time when Wolsey was not the decision maker, it took a long time for the intention to become the deed. Although Wolsey was the *de facto* chief minister by the middle of 1514, it was not until the next year that Henry was prepared to request the resignation of Archbishop Warham, the current lord chancellor, and to appoint Wolsey in his place. But the wait had been worthwhile for the cardinal. It would now be very difficult for anybody to challenge his decisions successfully, because Wolsey now had direct control of the legal system of the state.

2 Wolsey's Powers

It has often been maintained that Wolsey was in practice a dictator. There are powerful arguments to support this claim, although it must be remembered that in secular matters he could always be overruled (and sometimes was when Henry decided to grant the wishes of his friends) by the king. But such royal interventions were certain to be few and far between once it was well known that those who 'went behind the cardinal's back' and successfully secured the direct support of the king would be made to pay for their effrontery in the long run. For Wolsey was extremely vindictive in such circumstances and was relentless in his subsequent pursuit of those who had gained even a

Cardinal Wolsey

1 In his portrait Thomas Wolsey, Lord Chancellor of England and
Cardinal-Archbishop of York, looks like a man who had always
had it good. He must have been fifty when it was painted, and it
was an age when men aged fast. Even so his face is smooth and
5 unwrinkled. The jowls and neck are heavy and bull-like. But the
rest of the features are delicate to the point of effeminacy. The
lips are full, red and slightly pursed; while the eyebrows are
raised in quizzical interrogation. Something was just not so. But
whatever he was dissatisfied with, it was not himself.
10 (David Starkey, *The Reign of Henry VIII*)

slight temporary advantage over him. And the 'punishment' was always considerably in excess of the 'crime'. Financial ruin could be brought to a family when one of its members was reported to have said something unflattering about Wolsey in the hearing of the king.

What was the nature of this normally effective dictatorship in secular matters? As with most dictatorships, it struck randomly and depended on fear for its success. But it was certainly not a totalitarian dictatorship of the twentieth century type. The vast majority of the population were completely untouched by it, for Wolsey was not concerned about what they thought, said or did, as long as they did not cross him. The ones who suffered from the cardinal's activities were those who found themselves at odds with Wolsey's purpose. Often they would be innocent bystanders who happened to be in the wrong place at the wrong time, and who were required to make some sacrifice in order to further one of the minister's projects. It might be a matter of selling a piece of property that Wolsey needed for some purpose, or making an interest-free loan with no agreed date for repayment, or withdrawing from a legal case that Wolsey would find inconvenient. Those who were unwise enough to raise some objection to what was required of them would find themselves in considerable difficulties. If they were 'unimportant' people they might find themselves imprisoned on trumped up charges, with nobody prepared to listen to their side of the story. If they were more influential they might find a complicated and expensive law suit started against them, which was guaranteed to drain their resources of both time and money. They might even find the verdict in a law suit that they had already won reversed on Wolsey's personal authority in order to punish them for some lack of co-operation.

Not even the most powerful in the land were safe from the cardinal's vengeance – at least in the long term. Nobody who had offended him could sleep peacefully in their beds at night, because they did not know when they might be called to account for some seemingly innocent action they had taken. It was widely believed at the time that the disgrace and execution of the Duke of Buckingham, one of the leading nobles in the land, in 1521 (see page 74) happened because Wolsey wished to seek revenge on him for the scornful way he had been treated in the past. Although it is now clear that Buckingham had left himself open to treason charges by the careless things he had said, the suspicion remains that he would have remained safe had Wolsey not engineered the king's displeasure against him. By the early 1520s an established fact of political life in England was that you did not incur the cardinal's displeasure if you held any aspirations for the future. For, whereas he was known to be kind and generous to those who acknowledged his social and political superiority, he was equally renowned for the vigour with which he sought to redress for even an imagined slight. The fact that retribution was often slow in coming, and appeared to be totally unconnected with any original incident, made it all the more to be feared. Even those who had never suffered at his hands were fearful that one day they might.

* Wolsey's dictatorship in ecclesiastical matters came to be even more complete than it was in secular affairs. Once he had acquired the title *legatus a latere* for life there was nothing, in practice, that anybody could do to limit his powers over the Church in England. Although it was technically possible to appeal over his head to Rome, such were the difficulties in doing so that it was not a realistically available option for his opponents. So Wolsey was effectively free to do what he liked in spiritual affairs. However, his interventions were on a surprisingly narrow front, almost exclusively having to do with the appointment to clerical posts and the levying of fees for the provision of services. He made very little use of his sweeping powers either to reform abuses (perhaps because he was the principal culprit himself) or to prevent the spread of heresy (possibly because he attached so little importance to what people actually believed).

He successfully claimed the right to nominate whomever he wished to any clerical vacancy when it arose. He even managed to 'create' additional vacancies by forcing incumbents to resign where it could be shown that there had been some technical flaw in their original appointments. It is almost certain that he was acting illegally in many cases but nobody could successfully challenge his actions. Those who tried found that they lost more than they had bargained for. Sometimes a preferment was used to reward one of his followers or the client of one of his supporters, but more often it was simply a matter of extracting the largest possible bribe from the person or institution that had the normal legal right to nominate to the post so that the appointment could be made as was desired. It was the Church courts' power to confer legality on wills by 'proving' them and to settle disputes over inheritances that provided Wolsey with his most profitable type of interference. He claimed that as *legatus a latere* he had the right to make all legal decisions relating to wills and inheritances, and he used all his other powers to make good his claim. Once he had overcome all opposition to his pretensions, he instituted what was in effect a ten percent inheritance tax for his personal profit.

Wolsey rapidly gained a well deserved reputation as a rapacious enforcer of all his rights. He worked long hours and with a close attention to detail in order to maintain an encyclopaedic knowledge of what was happening throughout the country, and especially in the affairs of the nation's leading families. But he would have been unable to carry out his extractions without a large band of informers and agents to provide him with evidence and to carry out his instructions. Although it is not possible to piece together a complete picture of his operations, enough information has survived for historians to be able to capture the flavour of what was happening. It is known, for instance, that rewards were paid to those who gave news of the impending death of any clerical postholder. This was vital information for Wolsey to have because his right to nominate to a position was only valid if it were implemented before the normal nominator had done so. He, therefore, needed to be the first to hear of any vacancy arising. In the circumstances it is not surprising that a few informants exercised an imagination that was far too lively, and that some churchmen heard of their own deaths when they were still in what they considered to be the peak of health! But in all the collection of money and the extraction of favours, physical violence was never employed. It was not necessary. Wolsey controlled both of the country's legal systems and thus could always act within the law, as he interpreted it, whenever he wanted to exert pressure on those who were reluctant to act as he wished. And he was completely unscrupulous in his manipulation of the law, transferring cases from one court system to another as best suited his purposes, in complete defiance of past practices and existing conventions. In the process he generated huge amounts of impotent rage among those who suffered from his actions. Rarely has a public servant created so many enemies.

3 Wolsey and the Maintenance of Power

Wolsey was a man who could not relax. He was incessantly active with seemingly no interests other than his work and the keeping up of appearances. All of his effort was concentrated on these two activities. Much of his time (several hours on most days) was devoted to building up and maintaining his power base, without which he would 'have been nothing'. Although he was rarely in the same place as the king, who spent a significant part of most years 'progressing' around the southern part of his kingdom, Henry featured in almost Wolsey's every thought. 'What should he be told and what should be hidden from him?' 'How could he best be persuaded to follow a particular line of policy?' 'What interpretation could be placed on his instructions so that they would not be in conflict with Wolsey's own wishes?' 'How could the influence of those who had close personal contact with him on a day-to-day basis be minimised?' 'How much could be got away with?'

Similarly concentrated thought needed to be given to his dealings with Rome at the times he was attempting to win a new concession for himself. But there the situation was more difficult. Not only was he attempting to influence people he did not know and whose individual quirks he could only guess at, but there was often a considerable time lag between one move in his campaign and a reaction to it. Several months could pass between the writing of a dispatch to Rome and the receipt of a reply upon which he could base decisions about his next move. It is no wonder that it sometimes took several years for even minimal progress to be made. But the need to consider Rome so carefully disappeared once the title of *legatus a latere* had been granted for life in 1524. Thereafter Wolsey normally treated his ecclesiastical superior with ill-disguised contempt, ignoring letters all together, or dealing with them in a dilatory and partial manner – that is, until he once again needed papal support, this time to facilitate the annulment of Henry's marriage to Catherine of Aragon.

4 Wolsey's Wealth

Apart from using his position either to gain additional powers or to protect his existing authority, Wolsey devoted most of his attention to the acquisition of wealth. In this he was uniquely successful. Despite the fact that insufficient evidence exists for an accurate assessment of his income to be made – which is hardly surprising considering the nature of many of his transactions – it is possible to describe his success in general and relative terms. By the end of his career he was by far the richest person (in terms of income rather than capital) in the country, apart from the king. His nearest rivals enjoyed an income of only about one tenth of his own, such was the dominance of his position. Although Henry received more money than his minister, much of the royal revenue was spent on running the government of the country, minimal as it was. In addition, the king had real discretion in the spending of only a small percentage of his income. So, in terms of disposable wealth, Wolsey was undoubtedly the richest man in England, with relative purchasing power that has never been equalled in the nation's history. All this had been achieved by a man who had started with nothing.

Where did Wolsey's income come from? Much less than half of it arose directly from the posts he held, although he had managed to lay his hands on a number of the highest paid positions in the country. The greater part of his income was derived from less easily quantified sources. Probably the largest amount came from the fees charged by the ecclesiastical courts (see page 53), but this cannot be certain because it is impossible to estimate with any degree of precision the amount Wolsey received each year in 'gifts'. There were certainly thousands of them, and each was typically about the amount that would keep a modest gentry family for a year, but their total cannot even be guessed at reliably.

* How did Wolsey use his massive annual income? Certainly he was neither a saver nor an accumulator of capital for the future. Although he had two surviving illegitimate children, he had no ambitions to found a dynasty, nor did he have any wish to further the interests of his family. His thinking about the future was entirely self-centred and, as he did not envisage a situation in which he would step down from his position of power, there was no retirement to be provided for. He did not make provision for even his closest followers, so that when he was suddenly stripped of his possessions in 1529, most of his clients were left in dire financial straits. Their master's expenditure had all been on the here and now. But Wolsey was not a wastrel who indulged in 'having a good time'. He seemingly derived little pleasure from physical gratification. His pleasures were almost totally in the mind, and the greatest of these was thinking himself and being treated as the equal of kings. His vanity was unbounded and his income was used almost exclusively to satisfy it. The palaces he created at huge expense (Hampton Court was only the most famous of his four main residences) were not designed for his own comfort. They were planned to show the world what a great man he was, and to provide settings for the acting out of his public life.

He was determined that his court should be the equal to any in Europe, although he had to take care not to offend his king by outshining him too obviously. There is conflicting evidence about the size of Wolsey's household at the height of his power in the 1520s. At the very least it was made up of 500 people, ranging from noblemen to menial servants, and it may be that double that number were in attendance for special occasions. This places his court in the same range of those of his two masters, Henry VIII and the Pope. The daily routines were as would have been found in royal courts of the time, and the clothes and furnishings on display were as lavish as could be found anywhere. The collection of gold and silver vessels that could be in use or on show during the reception of important visitors, including the king, was sufficient to induce envy in all who saw it. No expense was spared in providing celebrations, especially for foreign envoys who could be relied upon to spread abroad full accounts of the splendours they had witnessed. On one such occasion he instructed his officers

1 to spare neither expense nor labour, to make the French such triumphant cheer that they might not only wonder at it here, but also make a glorious report in their country, to the King's honour and that of his realm.

The most extravagant gifts were given on such occasions so that evidence of great wealth could be paraded widely, in an age when the mighty were judged by the favours they were able to bestow.

Wolsey was at even greater pains to maintain his grandeur whenever he appeared before the general public, and especially when he undertook a journey. When setting out on a diplomatic venture into Europe he was particularly lavish in his preparations, providing his attendants with outfits of sufficient quality to convince onlookers of his great importance.

1 Then marched he forward out of his house at Westminster, passing through all London, over London Bridge, having before him of gentlemen a great number, three in a rank, in black velvet

livery coats and the most part of them with great chains of gold
5 about their necks. And all his yeomen, with noblemen's and
gentlemen's servants, following him in French tawny livery coats,
having embroidered on the backs and breasts of the same coats
these letters 'T' and 'C' under the cardinal's hat. His sumpter
mules, which were twenty in number and more, with his carts
10 and other carriages of his train, were passed on before, conducted
and guarded with a great number of bows and spears. He rode
like a cardinal, very sumptuously, on a mule trapped with
crimson velvet upon velvet, and his stirrups of copper and gilt;
and his spare mule following him with like apparel. And before
15 him he had his two great crosses of silver, two great pillars of
silver, the great seal of England, his cardinal's hat, and a
gentleman who carried his valaunce (otherwise called a cloak-bag)
which was made altogether of fine scarlet cloth embroidered over
and over with cloth of gold very richly, having in it a cloak of fine
20 scarlet.

Although convention dictated that as a churchman Wolsey rode on a
mule rather than fine horse, he more than made up for any lack of
grandeur that this might imply by the cavalcade that preceded him.
The two great crosses of silver (one because of the legateship he
possessed as the Archbishop of York and one because he was *legatus a
latere*) and the two great pillars of silver (indicating that he was a
cardinal) had become his hallmark. So also had the fact that he was
accompanied by a large number of 'tall and comely' yeoman to give
added dignity to his procession. He was so keen on having servants who
could impress by their bearing that anybody who recommended one to
him was sure to receive a reward that befitted his status.

'The Cardinal's Progress'

5 Wolsey and the Government of England

Wolsey was Henry VIII's chief minister for 15 years and historians have been generally disappointed by how little he achieved in domestic affairs. The orthodox interpretation has been that he devoted most of his attention to foreign affairs, to establishing and maintaining his personal power and to increasing his income. The implication has been that he should have been reforming and modernising the way the realm was governed, as Thomas Cromwell was to do (see pages 95–105). But perhaps this expectation reveals an anachronistic attitude towards the purposes of government in early sixteenth century England. Although leading humanists throughout western Europe were arguing the case for radical changes in both the aims and the methods of government, the vast majority of leading figures in public life expected very little of the royal government. They wished it to keep things much as they were (a widespread belief in 'progress' was still several centuries in the future), and to maintain law and order if it were threatened by major public disorders. But they did not wish it to interfere in the normal course of events more than was absolutely necessary. There was little contemporary disappointment that Wolsey did not do more.

Wolsey has often been criticised for his attitude towards parliament. In particular he has been accused of attempting to dispense with its services altogether. This is an essentially accurate diagnosis of the situation, as during his period in power only two parliaments were summoned. This was in stark contrast to the situation in the generations to either side of him, when parliament met for at least a short session in many years. But Wolsey made no secret of his dislike of an institution which almost seemed to be designed to stir up trouble for the government, and whose members appeared never to understand that their prime function was to carry out the king's wishes. After a bad experience in 1515, he only acted against his better judgement and allowed a parliament to be summoned in 1523 because it was obvious to him that there was no other way of raising the large sum of money that Henry needed to implement his forward policy in Europe. If he could have found some way of avoiding the necessity he would have done so, but his subsequent experience with the Amicable Grant (see page 42) confirmed that a vote from parliament was the only practical way of securing the additional funds required to pay for a large army.

 * Yet, minimal as was Wolsey's input into improving the state of England, it would be incorrect to suggest that he contributed nothing. A case could be made that he seriously attempted to bring greater justice to the English legal system. The issue was the balance of influence between two systems of law. The common law was the system that had enjoyed a dominant position in England since before the Norman Conquest. Civil (or equity) law was the system derived from the practices of the Roman Empire. It was in vogue in most of southern

Europe, and was used in the courts in England that were based on the king's person (especially the king's council when it acted as a court of law). Civil law was much favoured by the forward-looking elements in English society because it placed an emphasis on natural justice in decision making, rather than on precedent (what had been done before), which was the basic approach of the common law. It was felt in advanced circles that, although the common law protected litigants from partiality on the part of the judges by forcing them to reveal the reasoning, based on past practice, for their judgements, it did lead to some unjust verdicts where the party in the wrong could win a case on a technicality.

As Lord Chancellor, Wolsey was the head of the country's secular legal system and was directly responsible both for the legal work of the king's council and for the courts that had originated from it, such as Star Chamber and Chancery. He devoted a considerable amount of time and attention to this aspect of his responsibilities, hearing many cases himself and often taking care to make public the reasons for his decisions. However, it is clear that he was unscrupulous in using the system to further his own interests, especially by overturning common law decisions that adversely affected him and by using the law to harry those against whom he had a grudge. The most frequently quoted example of this, although doubt has been cast on its authenticity, is his treatment of Sir Amyas Paulet. Sir Amyas had incurred his passionate hatred by treating him with contempt (including having him put in the stocks) when he entered his first benefice as an arrogant and overbearing young man who many thought deserved to be cut down to size. When, more than a decade later, Wolsey became Lord Chancellor, he was swift to exact a spiteful revenge. He summoned his enemy to appear before him, and kept him waiting in daily attendance for more than five years under threat of the confiscation of all his property for contempt of court if he left London without permission. Wolsey used him as a very public reminder of what would happen to those who caused him offence, and as living proof that his memory was as long as it needed to be.

Yet personal satisfaction was certainly not his only motive in his legal work. He seems genuinely to have desired to see justice better served in the land, both by advancing civil law at the expense of common law and by ensuring that the courts for which he was directly responsible were accessible to the poor and the weak, who stood little chance of maintaining their rights against the rich and the strong in the common law courts, where the ability to pay large legal fees was normally an essential component of success. Thus he took pleasure in calling cases into one of his own courts when he learnt that a common law verdict had gone against what he considered to be natural justice, and he ensured that, especially in Star Chamber, cases in which restitution was being sought from the strong (except himself) were given an early hearing. He took most opportunities to try to convince the legal profession of the advantages of civil over common law. He is reported as having advised one senior official.

> 1 I counsel you and all other judges and learned men of his [the
>   king's] council to put no more into his head than law that may
>   stand with conscience; for when ye tell him this is the law, it were
>   well done ye should tell him also that although *this* be the law, yet
> 5 *this* is conscience; for law without conscience is not mete to be
>   given to a king by his council to be ministered by him nor by any
>   of his ministers: for every counsellor to a king ought to have a
>   respect to conscience before the rigour of the law . . . The king
>   ought for his royal dignity and prerogative to mitigate the rigour
> 10 of the law, where conscience hath the more force; and therefore in
>   his princely place he hath constituted a chancellor to order for
>   him the same. And therefore the court of the chancery hath been
>   commonly called the court of conscience; because it hath jurisdic-
>   tion to command the law in every case to desist from the
> 15 execution of the rigour of the same, whereas conscience hath most
>   effect.

However, it must be admitted that Wolsey was much less determined in the pursuit of justice for all than he was in furthering his own interests and that his interventions in cases probably caused more chaos than they did good. He attempted no institutional changes that would have ensured that his approach was continued once he was no longer available to champion them, and he was quick to abandon his support of the weak whenever matters that affected him personally demanded his attention. Gwyn laid great stress on the action he took against those who enclosed common land for personal profit, but, on balance, the evidence suggests that his approach was piecemeal and that he showed no determination to tackle the issue as a whole. The case in favour of Wolsey is also weakened by the alternative interpretations that can be put on many of his actions in this area. It can quite reasonably be maintained that his championing of the poor against the rich was merely a part of the vendetta against the nobility and gentry which he conducted against them as classes because he had so frequently been treated with contempt as a common and low born person by members of the social élites. It is perhaps significant that the one aspect of legal affairs that he conducted with consistent determination was the pro- secution of members of the nobility for breeches of the laws against maintenance and affrays. Although this was a vital part of any policy of upholding law and order, it also smacked of a strong desire to get even with those who thought of themselves as being his social superiors.

It has sometimes been suggested that Wolsey's attempts to reform the king's privy chamber show that he sought to make permanent improvements in the system of government he inherited. Particular attention has been paid to the Eltham Ordinances of 1526 which were aimed at regularising the chaotic finances of the privy chamber and which attempted to ensure more effective administration in the king's household. But a close examination of the circumstances leading up to the formulation of the ordinances, and of the way in which they were quickly allowed to lapse in all important respects, suggests that Wolsey's motives had little to do with more efficient administration and greater financial accountability. His prime concern was to reduce the scope that others had for influencing the king, and to increase the control that he could exercise over all aspects of government. The drive for greater efficiency was seen by all concerned to be no more than a ruse designed to make it appear that another piece of power seeking was an initiative designed to further the public interest. Once Wolsey had gained as much control as he could over the selection of the gentlemen who were to wait upon the king, the plans for an overhaul of the administrative procedures of the privy council were conveniently forgotten. Once again, Wolsey had shown that his domestic policies went little further than attempting to extend or consolidate his own position. Any idea of public service was largely foreign to him.

6 Wolsey and Henry VIII

Historians have, not surprisingly, been particularly interested in defining the nature of the relationship between Henry VIII and the cardinal. There has been considerable discussion of the extent to which Wolsey was able to operate independently of his sovereign's wishes, and of how far he was truly the servant of his royal master. There has also been a careful consideration of three further, closely related issues: how Wolsey was able to attain a position of dominance in Henry's favour, how he was able to maintain it for so long, and why he eventually lost it.

The political situation in England between 1514 and 1529 was very unusual. It appeared, somewhat paradoxically, as if a highly talented and independent-minded young king was very much under the influence of his wily, older minister. But, although this might at first sight seem to have been the situation, historians have generally been unprepared to accept that such was the case. While it is freely admitted that Wolsey became very skilful in manipulating others, it is maintained that he had met his match in Henry, who was more than able to look after himself in the hurly-burly of political intrigue and who was rarely fooled for long (and certainly not for 15 years). So the conclusion has usually been reached that Wolsey only enjoyed independent decision making when Henry was prepared to allow him to do so, or for short periods of time when the king was not properly aware of what was happening. Thus the relationship between the two was truly that of master and servant, even if the servant was occasionally allowed his

head to a greater extent than was normal in such hierarchical rela-
tionships. Possibly the most helpful analogy that has been used to
describe the situation is that of the senior management of a modern
large company in which Wolsey was the general manager making most
of the important day-to-day decisions, but where Henry was the
chairman who decided the policy objectives and devised the overall
strategy.

Both men certainly understood that Wolsey was completely dependent on the good will of his monarch and that if this were to be
withdrawn his position would be untenable. This was despite the fact
that Wolsey worked hard to establish an independent power base
within the Church, and felt at times that he had successfully created a
position for himself as the spiritual sovereign of England alongside
Henry's secular power. But in his heart of hearts he recognised that his
legateship *a latere* was only operable as long as Henry agreed that it
should be so. Therefore he was normally careful not to go against the
king's express wishes even in those aspects of ecclesiastical affairs where
theoretically he exercised ultimate authority within the country. On the
one occasion when he did, he had eventually to retract in abject
submission in the face of Henry's violent anger. The substance of the
incident was relatively petty – the appointment of an abbess to the
nunnery at Wilton in Wiltshire in 1528. Henry promised that the
nomination should go to one of his courtier's relations and informed
Wolsey accordingly. But Wolsey chose not to understand the instruction and awarded the post elsewhere. A second royal instruction was
ignored, and a third brought the response that the king's wishes had not
been clear. This was too much for Henry, who ranted that he was not
prepared to be treated in this way by his servant. Wolsey belatedly
recognised the seriousness of the situation and did everything possible
to placate his master. A great deal about the relationship between king
and minister was revealed in the process, as well as showing that
Wolsey was not immune from miscalculations on how much he could
get away with.

  * If the relationship was so dominated by Henry, then how was
Wolsey able to establish himself so powerfully in the first place? After
all, his position became such that Pollard felt able to describe him as
holding 'despotic authority in the state'. The answer is partly to be
found in the enormous range and extent of his abilities, and partly in
the personality and interests of Henry VIII. Wolsey was undoubtedly
one of the most able ministers of the crown in any period of British
history. Because of his very rare combination of exceptional brain
power, monumental drive and determination and a clear appreciation of
how to influence people, he was able to get things done that almost
everybody else would have found impossible. Henry was quick to
recognise that it was worth paying a high price in order to secure the
services of this exceptional man of business. He correctly assessed that,

however much power the minister amassed, there was no real danger that he could effectively challenge the king's position. England was a very hierarchical society and base-born subjects had never been able to survive in authority without the support of the monarch. There was no reason why Wolsey should be any different.

Wolsey also had another advantage in that he could be used to increase the distance between the king and the more mighty of his aristocratic subjects. Although the claim that Henry VIII was stongly motivated by a desire to eclipse the power of those nobles who could be seen as presenting a potential challenge to his régime has long been discredited, there can be no doubt that he enjoyed watching his leading subjects squirm as they were forced to yield pride of place to the son of a butcher who, because of his Church preferments, could demand precedence over them on all formal occasions. For Wolsey to be treated as the superior of the entire nobility of England, while being seen to be totally under the command of the king, meant that Henry could expect to be seen as even more exalted than he might otherwise have been.

Wolsey's explanation for his rise to prominence in the king's esteem was that he alone among the counsellors encouraged Henry to spend his time on his leisure pursuits and to leave the boring work of government to his ministers. Although this account is obviously less than the whole story, it does probably contain a germ of the truth. Henry was delighted to find somebody who could put his ideas into practice for him, without requiring constant instructions or supervision. Such an arrangement allowed him the best of all worlds: he could continue to live his life as he wished, without submitting himself overmuch to the discipline of work, while at the same time being confident that his wishes were generally being implemented.

* For Wolsey to achieve a position of dominance in the government was one thing: to retain it for a long period was something very different. It was the difference between climbing a high mountain and remaining camped there during all weathers. As a low-born chief minister serving a master who vigorously and successfully defended his habit of associating with whomsoever he wished, Wolsey had to accept that his motives and actions would be regularly misrepresented to the king by his numerous enemies – despite the fear of reprisal that he created in most people. Yet Wolsey managed to survive all attacks on his position for 15 years. This was truly a remarkable achievement. It happened both because of the minister's outstanding abilities and because the king was unusually shrewd in assessing the reliability of the information he was given. Thus the relationship between Henry VIII and Wolsey was a real (if very unequal) partnership that depended on the achievements of both parties for its success.

Contemporaries were so surprised by the length and extent of Wolsey's dominance that they were sometimes highly fanciful (to modern ways of thinking) in the explanations they gave for it. The most

commonly expressed opinion was that the cardinal exercised some form
of witchcraft over the king! But this was a perfectly reasonable
assumption, given the beliefs and understandings of the time. Polydore
Vergil, in his nearly contemporaneous account of the period, claimed
that Wolsey's long tenure of power was the result of his ability to
manipulate Henry:

1 Every time he wished to obtain something from Henry, he
  introduced the matter casually into his conversation; then he
  brought out some small present or another, a beautifully
  fashioned dish, for example, or a jewel or ring or gifts of that sort,
5 and while the King was admiring the gift intently, Wolsey would
  adroitly bring forward the project on which his mind was fixed.

There is no reason to doubt, despite the fact that Vergil was generally
critical of Wolsey, that the cardinal used techniques such as this. But
what is dubious is that they provide an explanation of the success of the
relationship. More recent analyses that stress the value that Henry saw
in Wolsey as a loyal and highly effective junior partner seem more
convincing.

  * In 1529 Henry decided to use the weapon against Wolsey that had
been available to him for more than a decade. A series of acts of
parliament in the fourteenth century had created the crime of *praemunire*, which in essence was any action taken to exercise papal powers in
England to the disadvantage of the king or any of his subjects. From the
time he had acquired his appointment as *legatus a latere* Wolsey had
clearly been open to a *praemunire* charge, and to the punishments
associated with it – the confiscation of all property and imprisonment
during the king's pleasure. However, when Henry decided to strike
down his minister is was not done decisively. Although Wolsey was
arrested and all his possessions were confiscated, he was released and
was allowed to live in modest comfort away from court. It was only
some months later that he was re-arrested and taken towards London
from his archdiocese of York, to which he had been 'exiled' by Henry.
But his health was broken and he died at Leicester on 29 November
1530. During the period of his disgrace he had done all he could to
engineer his reinstatement. He had sent a stream of pleading letters to
the king and had attempted to whip up support among his 'friends'
throughout Europe. But all had been to no avail. Henry had slowly
become convinced that his long-time leading servant must suffer the
only fitting end to his period of dominance – death as well as disgrace.
Wolsey's premature end at Leicester had in fact spared him from the
show trial and execution that almost certainly awaited him in London.
  Why had such a successful partnership ended so dramatically?
Undoubtedly, the major reason was Wolsey's failure to secure Henry
the annulment he desired of his marriage to Catherine of Aragon. It

seems that this was the issue at the forefront of the king's mind for the whole of the two years prior to Wolsey's fall. The minister had promised that this would be a matter easily resolved because of his influence with the papacy, from which all annulments of marriages must come, but every attempt had resulted in disappointment. (The question of the divorce is discussed at length in the parallel volume *Henry VIII and the Reformation in England*.) In the circumstances, Henry had been very patient. Anne Boleyn, his intended next wife, was maintaining her virtue in the face of Henry's every endeavour until he could guarantee to make 'an honest woman' of her, to her monarch's obvious frustration. And Henry was increasingly aware that the passage of time was endangering his aspiration to leave a male heir of adult years behind him when he died. It is an indication of the depth of Henry's faith in Wolsey and the skill with which the minister explained away the delays that the show-down was so long delayed. With anybody else it would have happened much earlier.

Historians have disagreed about why the king decided to act against his favourite minister when he did. Although the evidence is far from conclusive, the most plausible explanation appears to be that Henry decided to dispense with Wolsey when he became convinced by Anne Boleyn and her faction that the cardinal was actively conspiring to delay a papal decision – in the hope that the king would tire of his romantic pursuit in the meantime and would be prepared to return to Catherine – thus avoiding the political inconvenience of putting aside a wife who was widely admired and supported at home and abroad. Of course, it can never be known how much truth there was to this claim (although it is certain that there was some), but Henry seems to have come to believe it, and to have acted on the basis of it. However, the fact that on several occasions during the remaining months of his life Wolsey was given tokens of the king's continuing good will indicates that Henry was not entirely convinced of his minister's faithlessness, and that several times he seriously considered reinstating him in some way. That he did not give way to his doubts was a result of the skill with which the Boleyn faction constantly fed him with anti-Wolsey propaganda. Thus it seems highly probable that there was considerable truth in the contemporary claim that the cardinal was the victim of his political enemies, led by Anne Boleyn. But, although Wolsey's unpopularity was so great that there was general rejoicing at his removal from power, Henry was realistic enough soon to regret that he had allowed himself to be persuaded to destroy the servant who was better able to carry out his wishes than was anyone else then available to him. Wolsey may not have been very likeable, but he was certainly a great man according to the criteria most frequently used when such judgements are made. However, many will conclude that a person of outstanding ability who acted in such a self-centred manner throughout most of his life was indeed a wastrel rather than being a man who deserves our admiration.

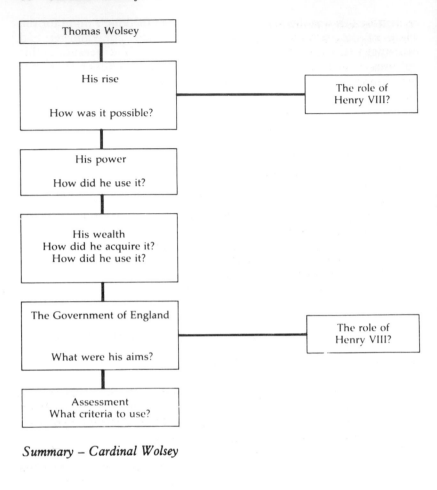

Summary – Cardinal Wolsey

Making notes on 'Cardinal Wolsey'

When making your notes on this chapter – which can afford to be fairly detailed – you should have three questions in mind throughout. These are: i) what were Wolsey's aims? ii) what were his methods? and iii) how successful was he in achieving his aims? But, unless you are a very experienced note-maker, you are unlikely to be able to organise what you write under these headings. You may be better advised to make your notes following the structure of the chapter, and to draw out your answers to the three questions afterwards.

The following headings, sub-headings and questions could well provide you with an appropriate framework for your notes.

1.   Rise to Pre-eminence
1.1. Why was he able to rise to the top?
1.2. What positions did he hold?
2.   Wolsey's Powers
2.1. secular
2.2. clerical
2.3. What were his methods?
3.   Wolsey and the Maintenance of Power
      What strategies did he employ?
4.   Wolsey's Wealth
4.1. income (size and sources)
4.2. expenditure
5.   Wolsey and the Government of England
      Why did he spend so much time and energy on the Star Chamber?
6.   Wolsey and Henry VIII
6.1. What was the nature of their relationship?
6.2. Why was Wolsey so powerful?
6.3. Why did the relationship last so long?
6.4. Why did the relationship come to an end?

Answering essay questions on 'Cardinal Wolsey'

In preparing to answer essay questions about Thomas Wolsey it is important to think about his political life as a whole. You will therefore need to use the ideas you have developed and the information you have acquired from reading both of the last two chapters.
   Look at the following questions:
   1. Why has Wolsey's career given rise to such different assessments?
   2. How distinctive were Wolsey's aims and achievements in foreign policy?
   3. How far did Wolsey achieve the objectives of his foreign policy?
   4. To what extent did Wolsey deserve to be generally unpopular?
   5. On what principles was Wolsey's foreign policy based?
   6. 'Despite his great power Thomas Wolsey left little permanent mark on English history.' Discuss.
   7. Was Thomas Wolsey successful?
   8. 'Unrealistic and unpopular.' Is this a fair assessment of Wolsey's foreign policy?
   9. How far should Wolsey be blamed for the policies he followed?
      Which of the questions require you to use material from both chapter 3 and chapter 4? Which of these questions asks you to undertake a general assessment of Wolsey's achievements?
   You will remember that a vital part of preparing to tackle an essay

question based on an assessment of anything is consciously to identify the criteria you will use in making your judgement. It is best to state these explicitly in your essay. What criteria would you employ in assessing Wolsey's success?

Look at question 4. A successful answer to this question also depends on the identification of criteria. What criteria are these? In preparing to answer several other of the questions it would be helpful (but not essential) to identify criteria. Which questions are these? Prepare a plan for an answer to question 9 based on criteria you have identified.

Source-based questions on 'Cardinal Wolsey'

1 Wolsey's Portrait
Study Wolsey's portrait (page 51) and the conclusions that David Starkey has drawn from it (page 51). Answer the following questions.
a) Which one of Starkey's conclusions do you find most convincing? Explain your answer. (5 marks)
b) Which one of Starkey's conclusions do you find least convincing? Explain your answer. (5 marks)
c) Discuss the view that 'portraits of historical figures provide useful evidence, but least of all about the personality and character of the sitter'. (10 marks)

2 Wolsey makes an impression (1)
Carefully read Wolsey's instructions to his officers (page 56). Answer the following questions.
a) What was Wolsey's stated reason for wanting to impress the French envoys? (2 marks)
b) Explain the significance of the phrase 'the king's honour' (line 3). (4 marks)
c) Why did Wolsey want to create an impression wherever he went? (4 marks)

3 Wolsey makes an impression (2)
Carefully read the description of Wolsey setting out on a diplomatic mission (pages 56–7) and study the illustration of a similar event (page 57). Answer the following questions.
a) In the contemporary account what is meant by i) 'livery coats' (line 4), and ii) 'sumpter mules' (line 8)? (2 marks)
b) Indicate four ways in which the procession was intended to impress those who saw it. (4 marks)
c) What was the probable aim of the artist who executed the

illustration? What evidence is there to support your contention? (*3 marks*)

d) For what reasons is the illustration unlikely to be accurate in matters of detail? Identify four ways in which the account and the illustration do agree with one another. (*6 marks*)

4 Wolsey and Henry VIII

Carefully read the extract from Polydore Vergil given on page 64. Answer the following questions.

a) What internal evidence does the extract contain to suggest that, despite the author's known hostility to Wolsey, it is not a complete fabrication? (*4 marks*)

b) This section of Vergil's *History* was not published until after Henry VIII's death. What were the probable reasons for this? (*4 marks*)

c) Would you judge this extract to be completely reliable? Explain your answer. (*7 marks*)

CHAPTER 5

Henry VIII and the Control of his Subjects

1 Introduction

There are two popular perceptions of Henry VIII in general circulation. He tends either to be thought of as 'Bluff King Hal', the happy-go-lucky pleasure seeker who was always the life and soul of the party, or to be remembered as a despotic and bloodthirsty tyrant who ordered heads to be cut off at the least sign of opposition (see page 5). In his dealings with his subjects, it is the latter image that probably most closely approaches reality – although it is of course a gross oversimplification and therefore a long way from the truth.

It appears that throughout his life Henry reacted strongly whenever his will was opposed or whenever his instructions were not carried out to his satisfaction. Although he was easily distracted from his rages by activities such as hunting when he was a young man, his temper was less easily calmed and grudges were more deeply harboured as he grew older. Yet his anger was rarely uncontrolled for more than a few hours. He was nearly always quick to re-assert the dominance of his intellect over his emotions and to allow his shrewd political judgement rather than his feelings of annoyance to direct his actions. But this did not mean that he was prepared to forgive and forget: merely that he was prepared to wait for the right moment to exact his revenge. The wait could be a long one. It was not unknown for a decade or more to elapse before full vengeance was taken. In this he was curiously similar to the most famous of his ministers.

Henry often gave the appearance of being at heart a bully, and one who, like most bullies, was most vicious to those who were most frightened of him. He was also savage with those who seemed disdainful of him or whom he imagined had offered him the least insult. The only people who were able to frustrate his wishes and to continue to thrive (at least for the time being) were those who were skilful enough to treat him with abject deference when necessary, while pursuing their point of view with a determination that matched Henry's own. But personalities such as Thomas Wolsey and Anne Boleyn are few and far between in any age, and the vast majority of Henry's subjects were totally unable to mount an effective resistance to any of their monarch's wishes. And the more Henry got his own way, the more he expected to do so. Therefore, it is accurate to think of him in his final years as hating opposition almost to the point of madness. Although he was never as arbitrary as to say 'Off with their heads', it is not ridiculous to imagine that he might have done so!

Yet Henry was never a real tyrant, ruling his domains in whatever way his fancy took him. His actions were consistent with both the generally accepted contemporary view of the nature of kingship and a clearly formulated theory of the duties of the subject. Henry, along with most of his subjects, believed that a king was God's lieutenant on earth, charged with punishing those who broke His commandments. It was only for God to pass judgement on the actions of his lieutenant – mere mortals were guilty of wicked presumption if they attempted to do so. The subject's duty, therefore, was to honour and obey his king, because to do otherwise would be to act contrary to God's wishes. This duty remained even if, in the subject's opinion, the king acted unjustly, for it was not the role of ordinary people to dispute the monarch's decisions about what was just. Nor was it convincing for those who wished to challenge any of Henry's actions to argue their case on the basis of 'illegality'. While it is true that the 'rule of law' was an important component of English life, few contested the assumption that the law was the king's law. It was generally agreed that he was above it, and was, therefore, not controlled by it. The fact that he chose to gain the support of his leading subjects to all new laws by having them passed as acts of parliament did not undermine this principle. Nor was the fact that he chose to punish most (but not all) erring subjects by 'due process of law'. These actions merely displayed his virtue in taking special care to act as a good master towards his subjects.

  * Surprising as it may seem to modern readers, these views were strongly supported by a large majority of Henry's subjects. To many it was a moral question (right or wrong) rather than a matter of expediency. However, there were also compelling selfish reasons for all but the poorest members of society to accept the prevailing orthodoxy. It was widely seen as being the only safeguard against anarchy, as an essential element in the protection of rights and property from the ravages of the poor who were often strong and envious and who, therefore, needed to be kept firmly in their place. Thus even those with few possessions (but more than none) tended to support the existing *status quo*. They may not have liked the way in which the king sometimes took advantage of them (especially in levying taxation) but they normally regarded it as the lesser of all evils. This, of course, was especially so of the well-to-do sections of the community, such as the tens of thousands of landlords large and small, who depended for much or all of their income on the rents paid by their tenants. It was Henry's expectation that they would take positive action to uphold the king's law whenever disorder threatened. And he was rarely disappointed.

  Given these circumstances, it was not surprising that any monarch should regard opposition as a sin – 'naughty', which in the sixteenth century was a synonym for evil, was the word most used by contemporaries. And given Henry's massively high opinion of himself, it should surprise no-one that he of all monarchs regarded most forms of opposition as deserving the death penalty. Historians have often used the fact that in the 1530s high treason was redefined by act of parliament to include almost every criticism of the king, whether spoken or in writing, as evidence of Henry's despotism, but it was no more than a logical extension of prevailing assumptions. Henry was more thorough in protecting his position than many of his predecessors had been, but he was not attempting to change the essential relationship between the monarch and his subjects.

2   Henry VIII, the Nobility and the White Rose Party

Nor is it to be wondered at that Henry's special fury was reserved for any opposition that seemed to challenge his right to be king. After all, he was the son of a man who had won the crown on the field of battle, and whose right of inheritance was not beyond dispute. However, he was fortunate in one respect: most of those who could claim a right to succeed because of their royal blood had died or had been executed before his accession. But this did not stop him being almost paranoid about the few who remained. He inherited the leading figure of the 'White Rose Party' (as the relatives of the Yorkist line, that Henry VII had replaced, were popularly known) as a prisoner when his father died. Edmund de la Pole was the son of one of Edward IV's sisters, and thus had a very respectable claim to the throne. As his only brother, Richard, was already fighting alongside the French, it was obvious to Henry that the 'Yorkist card' would be played by his enemies whenever war with France was resumed. He therefore ordered Edmund's execution in 1513, just to make certain that there would be no potential focus for opposition while he was absent from the realm, leading an army into France. But, of course, this did not remove the problem. Richard de la Pole remained at liberty, and was even recognised as Richard IV by the King of France. While Richard lived Henry felt that he was occupying a potentially contested throne. And it was not until 1525 that the threat was removed, when Richard de la Pole became one of the 'French' casualties at the battle of Pavia (see page 41). In the meantime, Henry's sense of insecurity remained.

Undoubtedly, the existence of the Yorkist threat, however remote it might be, reinforced Henry's deep suspicion of anyone who enjoyed high social standing and great wealth independently of him. His fear was that such people could easily abandon their loyalty to him in order to support any pretender who emerged. He was particularly anxious about those who did not appear to accept his will unreservedly, even if they had a previously unblemished record of acquiescence. It is probable that Henry projected onto others his own unscrupulous and self-seeking attitudes, because his suspicions were frequently much greater than the evidence warranted. In 1520 he even took the extraordinary step of instructing Wolsey in writing (such things were rarely committed to paper) to keep a close watch on leading members of

Those with royal blood alive during the reign of Henry VIII

There were no direct descendants of the Norman kings of England. All those who claimed royal blood were indirectly descended from Edward III (1327–77).

The House of Lancaster

The Tudors were the last remaining branch of the House of Lancaster, which was descended from Edward III's fourth son, John of Gaunt. Henry VIII was a fifth generation descendant, via one female line.

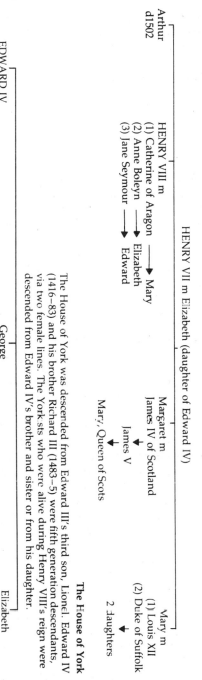

The House of York

The House of York was descended from Edward III's third son, Lionel. Edward IV (1416–83) and his brother Richard III (1483–5) were fifth generation descendants, via two female lines. The York sits who were alive during Henry VIII's reign were descended from Edward IV's brother and sister or from his daughter.

(x = executed by Henry VIII)

the nobility as he doubted their loyalty. Among those named was his closest friend, Henry Brandon, Duke of Suffolk. Henry must have been feeling very disturbed to encourage Wolsey to concoct a case against one of his leading supporters. And, of course, Wolsey needed little encouragement to try to humiliate any of the great nobles who so regularly took pleasure in belittling him as a social upstart. However, Suffolk had done nothing that could reasonably be interpreted as treason. The Duke of Buckingham (one of the others named in Henry's note) was not so fortunate. He was not only a great magnate, controlling what was almost an independent state in the Marcher Lordships between England and Wales, but he was also known to be sympathetic to the White Rose Party. In such circumstances, he had been particularly unwise to express the opinion in private conversation that Henry might not be king for much longer. Once Wolsey had received reports from Buckingham's servants of this and of other similar indiscretions, there was little likelihood that punishment would be escaped. In early 1521 Buckingham was ordered to London, was arrested and imprisoned in the Tower, was tried and found guilty by his peers, and was executed. Few were slow to learn the lesson that careless talk really could cost lives.

Buckingham died essentially because he was unprepared to act publicly as if he accepted that the king was his superior in all respects. But even those who cringed before Henry were equally unsafe if their social position was thought by him to pose a threat. The Percy family, as Earls of Northumberland, had exercised a virtually independent jurisdiction in north-eastern England for several centuries. Henry was determined that this should cease. He therefore sought a pretext on which to take action against the family. But its head was so timid that nothing he said or did could even be misinterpreted to suggest disloyalty. Yet this was not good enough for Henry. If it were not possible to mount a treason trial, other ways must be found to destroy the family's fortune. In the end, after a lengthy campaign of intimidation, the earl, having no children of his own (although there were brothers to succeed him), was persuaded to name the king as his heir. Thus, when he died in 1537, the Percy lands reverted to the crown, and one of the few families that could claim great distinction in its own right had been humbled.

However, it was the White Rose Party which continued to cause concern to Henry even after the death of Richard de la Pole in 1525. Although the remaining potential contenders for the throne were only distantly related to the former Yorkist kings, there was still the possibility that they might act as the focus of opposition to the Tudors. The leading members of the White Rose Party were now the three Pole brothers (totally separate from the recently extinct de la Pole family), who inherited their claim from their mother, the Dowager Countess of Salisbury, the daughter of Edward IV's brother. The Cavendish family,

to dissolve the hundreds of smaller monasteries that had acquired such a bad general reputation for religious and moral laxity over the previous decades, and for their property (goods and land) to be handed over to the king. This action, the significance of which sunk in when commissioners arrived in the locality to drive out the monks and nuns, to take possession of their goods and to lease out their lands, was furiously resented in many areas. It seems that the general view was that outsiders had arrived to rob them of an important part of their heritage and that it was an outrageous piece of legalised theft. Some historians have been unprepared to believe that these events could have stirred such violent passions, and have suggested that there must have been more important causes for the major uprising that followed. But such views fly in the face of most of the evidence, and are in danger of being based on twentieth century value systems rather than those of the time. Although it is not always easy for us to accept it, there is little doubt that many sixteenth century Englishmen were more moved by issues of right and wrong than by matters affecting their material well-being. This is not to claim that there were no significant economic and social causes of the uprisings of 1536–7, but merely to suggest that these were probably of peripheral rather than central importance.

5 The Pilgrimage of Grace

The widespread revolt that took place in late 1536 and lasted into early 1537 is known as the Pilgrimage of Grace. It is probably the best documented of all early modern popular uprisings. Many of the major figures wrote detailed accounts of what happened, and there is good reason to regard these highly in terms of both completeness and accuracy. They were composed by intelligent and honourable men who believed that it would be in their best interests to tell the truth. In addition, a large number of the letters written at the time by the leading participants have been preserved, and from them it is possible to chart the shifting perceptions and attitudes of the writers as events unfolded. The major work on these sources was carried out by two sisters, Madeleine and Ruth Dodds, in the years before the First World War. The resulting two volume history of *The Pilgrimage of Grace and the Exeter Conspiracy*, published in 1915, is a fascinating, detailed account of what happened and it is unlikely ever to be bettered. It is a splendid piece of research. However, this does not mean that the Dodds are to be relied on throughout. While there is little justification for challenging their description of what happened, there is plenty of reason to suggest that the conclusions they reached about causes, motives and consequences are questionable in places. These, of course, rely very much on the interpretation of and extrapolation from evidence, rather than on its more straightforward use to compile a chronological narrative, and are therefore likely to be disputed as being matters of opinion rather than matters of fact. There is much more certainty about the facts of the case.

   * Although it is only strictly accurate to use the phrase 'Pilgrimage of Grace' to describe the uprising in Yorkshire between October and December 1536, the term is normally applied to all the insurrections that took place in the north of England in 1536 and 1537. The first stage might most appropriately be called the Lincolnshire Uprising of October 1536. It was over in little more than a fortnight (from the 2nd to the 18th), but while it lasted it was extremely threatening to the government. What made it so was that it was not just a disturbance caused by the 'commons'. It was certainly led, and was perhaps instigated, by well-to-do landowners, who would normally have been relied upon by the government to quell discontent rather than to encourage it. But not all the gentlemen who took part in the rising did so voluntarily. The rebels seized all the members of the gentry they could find and threatened them with loss of life and property if they did not join them. Few were brave enough to stand up to such intimidation, or alert enough to make good their escape before they were captured. As a result, it very quickly became apparent to the king and his council that troops from other parts of the country would have to be brought in to put down the uprising. Even if musters could have been called out in the area, it is probable that they would have sided with the rebels.

   Within a few days of the initial disturbance about 40,000 Lincolnshire men (mainly from the areas around Louth and Horncastle) had responded to the rebels' call to arms, spread by word of mouth as well as by the lighting of beacons and the ringing of church bells. They were generally well-armed and well-disciplined – it was really a very unofficial but very enthusiastic muster. They marched to Lincoln where they were welcomed by the majority of the city's population. But they were not as united as they seemed. Most of the gentlemen, whether volunteers or pressed men, had become fearful that they had exposed themselves to destruction. They had much to lose and it seemed that they were heading towards the point where they would forfeit everything. They knew that the Duke of Suffolk, with loyal troops, was making good speed towards them and they could not foresee a situation in which they could be finally victorious if fighting commenced. They might defeat one army, but to what purpose? Their desire was to persuade Henry to reverse some of his more unpopular policies, just as he had abandoned the Amicable Grant in 1525. It was not to enter on a lengthy civil war. They therefore seized on the first informal offer that was made them – that if they dispersed peaceably their demands would be considered by the king. Although some of the more hot-headed of the commons threatened to kill the gentlemen for betraying them, they were unable to win over the majority of their colleagues to a continuation of the uprising. Hence, by the time Suffolk and his troops arrived at Lincoln, there was no organised resistance to be overcome. There was merely a simmering discontent that Henry was in no mood to mollify.

The king's initial reaction to the news of the uprising was predictable. He instructed that the rebellion should be crushed with the maximum of force and with the subsequent execution of all those who could be identified as having taken part. His reasoning was straightforward. The rebels had failed in their primary duty of loyalty to their monarch and they therefore deserved to die. There could be no extenuating circumstances, for the slight to his honour must be avenged in full. His attitude is well illustrated by the reply to the rebels' demands that he wrote with his own hand. It began:

1 How presumptuous then are ye, the rude commons of one shire,
and that one of the most brute and beastly of the whole realm, and
of least experience, to find fault with your prince, for the electing
of his councillors and prelates; and to take upon you, contrary to
5 God's law, and man's law, to rule your prince, whom ye are
bound by all laws to obey, and serve, with both your lives, lands,
and goods, and for no wordly cause to withstand; the contrary
hereof you, like traitors and rebels, have attempted, and not like
true subjects, as ye name yourselves.

However, Henry was forced to wait many months for his intentions to be put even partially into effect. He had thought that his time of danger was over when he had received the news that the Lincolnshire rebels were disbanding. But much worse was to follow. Within days it became clear that a more serious rising was already under way a little further north in Yorkshire and that any vengeance would have to be postponed for the time being.

* The rising in Yorkshire was in many ways similar to that in Lincolnshire. It was made up of all the able-bodied men from whole communities led, willingly or under duress, by the local landowners. Troops were mustered and were given enough money to buy their own supplies, thus avoiding the need for theft. The money was raised as donations from the well-to-do, especially churchmen. An oath was administered to everybody in an attempt to protect the rising from treachery, for such was the generally accepted power of oath taking that few people were prepared to risk eternal damnation by failing to fulfil the terms of an oath that they had sworn. But the Yorkshire rising was different in one important respect: it enjoyed high quality leadership.

Robert Aske was rapidly recognised as the undisputed leader of the rebellion. Although he was a member of an important Yorkshire family and was thus operating in his own locality, his experience was of London as well as the north. He was a highly trained and able lawyer who was used to practising in the law courts of the capital. As might be expected, he had a considerable command of language and was skilled at handing himself in public debate. He was also a highly competent organiser. As a consequence, he did much to ensure that the rising was carefully co-ordinated and that the troops under his command were organised as an army rather than as an enthusiastic rabble. He was also responsible for ensuring that the rebels' actions were presented in the best possible light, so as to be acceptable to all sections of the community, without frightening the wealthy into their normal opposition to popular disturbances. It was Aske who coined and popularised the name 'Pilgrimage of Grace', which should strictly only be applied to the rising he led. This was more than a piece of clever public relations. It encapsulated the spirit of the rising as far as Aske was concerned, in that it identified the main purpose of the rebels – to undertake a journey that would yield them spiritual benefits. The hope was that, by a show of armed force, the Pilgrims would be able to persuade Henry that he should abandon his attacks on the Church (especially the dissolution of the monasteries) and should return to his previous loyalty to Rome. But Aske did not know quite how his purposes might be achieved. He assumed that Henry was really a caring monarch who had been misled by his wicked and low-born councillors, such as Thomas Cromwell, and who would change his policy when he realised that the cost of not doing so would be a bloody, civil war. It was, therefore, necessary for the Pilgrims to be prepared to fight if they had to, even though Aske and most of the other leaders believed that Henry would give way before that point was reached. It was Aske's efficient arrangement of his men in conventional army formations that turned the Pilgrimage of Grace into a particularly threatening uprising.

The essentials of Aske's approach were revealed in the form of the re-written Lincolnshire oath that he had copied many times (there were no printing presses in the north of England at the time) and sent to most districts to the north and west of him.

The Oath of the Honourable Men
1 Ye shall not enter into this our Pilgrimage of Grace for the Commonwealth, but only for the love that ye do bear unto Almighty God and his faith, and to Holy Church militant and the maintenance thereof, to the preservation of the King's person and
5 his issue, to the purifying of the nobility and to expulse all villein blood and evil councillors against the commonwealth from his Grace and his Privy Council of the same. And that ye shall not enter into our said Pilgrimage for no particular profit to your self, nor to do any displeasure to any private person, but by counsel of
10 the commonwealth, nor slay nor murder for no envy, but to your hearts put away all fear and dread, and take afore you the Cross of Christ, and in your hearts his Faith, the Restitution of the Church, the suppression of those Heretics and their opinions, by all the holy contents of this book.

The support for Aske was widespread. Starting in the East Riding of Yorkshire, the Pilgrimage was joined by numerous contingents from the rest of the county, from Durham and from Northumberland. Less support was forthcoming from the west of the Pennines (Lancashire, Cumberland and Westmorland), but it was not insignificant. While it is true that numbers of notional Pilgrims, especially from the dales of Northumberland, used the uprising as an excuse to pillage the property of their neighbours, the vast majority of the rebels behaved in a most restrained manner as they gathered first at York and then at Pontefract.

Pontefract was significant because it contained the castle that was theoretically a royal stronghold guarding the road south. In practice, the castle was anything but secure. It was in a very poor state of repair and was only garrisoned by about 300 troops – and their loyalty was thought to be highly suspect. They were under the command of Lord Thomas Darcy, within whose area of influence the town fell. Darcy was hardly a confirmed loyalist. In fact, for several years Henry had suspected him (without firm evidence) of conspiring with fellow nobles from the north, and possibly with the Imperial ambassador, to oppose the religious changes that were taking place. As a result, Darcy had regularly and until very recently been refused permission to leave London and to return to his estates in the north. The king's fear had been that, although Darcy was about 80 and beyond the stage when he could be expected to be actively involved in anything, his return to Yorkshire would act as a signal for a rebellion to begin. It is therefore not surprising that Henry did not believe Darcy's protestations that he had no connection with Aske and his Pilgrims, especially when he surrendered Pontefract Castle to them without the exchange of a single blow. Darcy's argument that he had had no alternative, as his stronghold was indefensible and his men were ready to desert, did not impress his monarch, who concluded that had Darcy not been in league with the rebels he would have put up what resistance he could. The fact that Darcy then joined the Pilgrims and become one of their most prominent leaders suggests that Henry's opinion was not far from the truth.

When Pontefract Castle surrendered on 21 October, there were about 35,000 well-armed and horsed Pilgrims under Aske's command. The king had very little with which to oppose them. The Earl of Shrewsbury was moving through the East Midlands towards them with a few thousand men and the Duke of Norfolk was hurrying north with a few thousand more. But even when these two forces met, the rebels would still outnumber them by three or four to one, and there was little prospect of further troops being made available speedily. The Pilgrims seemed to possess every military advantage. But, fortunately for the king, Aske and his fellow leaders still desperately hoped for a negotiated settlement. Therefore it was not difficult for Norfolk to reach agreement with the Pilgrims when he met their representatives on

Doncaster Bridge on 27 October. He won their confidence by appearing to sympathise with their demands, which was easy for him to do as he was reputed to be a conservative in religion and the political enemy of Thomas Cromwell and his supporters, whom the Pilgrims blamed for the king's unpopular policies. It was agreed that the Pilgrims would disband while Norfolk accompanied a deputation of rebels (excluding the best known leaders who would remain in Yorkshire to ensure the maintenance of law and order) to London to present their demands to the king.

However, Aske and his colleagues were not totally naïve. They realised that if the pressure were totally removed from Henry he would do nothing. They were therefore very careful to maintain their organisation in good order, although most of their men were sent back to their homes for the time being. But Henry was more than a match for Aske as a politician. He delayed providing the Pilgrims' envoys with an answer for several weeks in the hope that the uprising would lose its impetus in the meantime. And when it appeared that the Pilgrims' patience was running out, he played for even more time by asking for their demands to be clarified. He maintained that he had been presented with such generalised requests that he was not able to respond to them adequately. His instruction was that the Pilgrims' leaders should meet to draw up specific demands and to communicate these to him via the Duke of Norfolk. At the same time he ordered Norfolk to promise whatever was necessary in order to end the rebellion, already having decided that whatever promises were made need not be honoured because they had not been made by him personally and because they had been extorted under duress.

In early December the Pilgrims' leaders met in Pontefract and drew up their detailed demands in the form of 24 separate articles. Historians used to view these articles as the clearest evidence of the causes of the Pilgrimage. Their reasoning was that the Pilgrims' demands must have revealed their motives for rebelling. More recently it has been agreed that no such straightforward link exists, and that the inclusion of particular issues merely proves that one or more of the leaders felt strongly on the matter. After all, the Pilgrims were not limited in the number of demands they could make, so there was no point in one leader offending another by objecting to a demand he wanted to make, even if it represented a minority point of view. It is also seen as self-evident that as the articles were written exclusively by members of the social élites, they need not have reflected the views of the common people. Thus the articles are not now thought to be as historically significant as they once were.

Nevertheless, the articles can be used to illustrate many of the rebels' concerns. Nine of the demands had to do with religion. In total they added up to a request for the changes of the past few years to be reversed, and for the situation that had existed prior to 1531 to be restored. Six articles were political. They sought a similar reversal of recent changes and the punishment of those (Cromwell and his collaborators) who had initiated them. They also looked for a return to an imaginery 'golden age' when parliaments had been freely elected and had made decisions freely (without pressure from the king or his servants). Certainly the overall tenor of the articles is conservative and even reactionary. It is obvious that those who devised and agreed them were united in their dislike of the changes that had taken place in recent years. It also seems that they had not been greatly in favour of the situation that had existed throughout their adult lifetimes, and that they yearned for a return to an earlier age when central government had exerted little control beyond the Trent and when the north had been made up of a series of virtually independent fiefdoms.

As soon as the articles were ready, a group of 300 leading Pilgrims carried them to the Duke of Norfolk at Doncaster. An agreement was reached on 6 December. For the king's part it was promised that the details of the articles would be considered by a freely elected parliament which would probably be held at York in the near future, and that all the Pilgrims would be pardoned for their actions during the Pilgrimage. For their part the Pilgrims agreed to disband peaceably. Aske and his colleagues were in no doubt that they had won a great victory and that the causes of their discontent would soon be removed without more than a single life being lost – and that one fatality had been the result of an accident. A band of Pilgrims mistook one of their own men for an opponent because he was wearing the jerkin emblazoned with the cross of St George (the emblem of the king's troops) that he always donned for a muster and they attacked and killed him before the error could be explained.

* The leading Pilgrims' sense of exhilaration can largely be explained by the fact that Norfolk had managed to convince them that Henry was grateful to them for opening his eyes to what had been going on, and regarded them as having done a considerable service to the country. Aske, in particular, was totally persuaded of the king's good intentions. Within a month of the Doncaster agreement, he had travelled to London at Henry's request and had been received by his monarch with considerable honour. In what Aske interpreted as a spontaneous gesture of friendship, (it was really a calculated deception), Henry had even given him the heavy gold chain he had been wearing when they first met. He took at face value the king's request that he write down in detail all that had happened during the Pilgrimage so that his Council could be better informed about the opinions of the people. In reality Henry was carrying out a not very sophisticated confidence trick. He wished to win Aske's enthusiastic support so that there would be less likelihood of the rebellion flaring up again while he was making ready to regain military control of the north, and he wanted a detailed account of what had happened so that he would be able to identify the guilty

parties for future retribution. But Henry's 'act' was so good, and Aske's desire to believe him was so strong, that no suspicions were aroused. When Aske returned to Yorkshire later in January he acted as the king's most effective ambassador, calming the fears that many had about the unexpected delay in the return northwards of the Duke of Norfolk with the promised general pardon and the details of the parliament soon to be held.

But Norfolk was not sent north as a pacifier. He was left in no doubt by the king that his loyalty would be assessed according to the severity of his treatment of the rebels. As Norfolk knew that Henry suspected him of sympathising with the Pilgrims, he had every intention of acting so as to remove any doubts about his dependability. He was assisted by further outbreaks of disorder which, although they were condemned by most of the Pilgrims' leaders, could be used as an excuse for considerable repression. The most serious of the disturbances took place in Cumberland during February 1537. The commons, with virtually no gentry support, rose up and attacked the border stronghold of Carlisle. They were driven off with hundreds of casualites (the popularly rumoured figure of 800 dead seems improbable in the circumstances), and Norfolk was able to display his enthusiasm for vengeance by arranging for several hundred of those who were thought to have taken part to be hanged in their own villages as a warning that further resistance was pointless. But Henry had no intention of allowing Norfolk to feel secure. Within weeks he was writing him an angry letter accusing him of negligence for allowing some of the bodies of those hanged to be cut down for burial, rather than remaining as a grisly reminder of the consequences of rebellion for years to come. Not surprisingly, Norfolk felt that he was being unfairly blamed. But the ploy was successful, as the king's lieutenant in the north tried even harder to provide satisfaction to his royal master.

Henry and Cromwell judged that, as Norfolk seemed well enough established to be able to crush any further resistance, the time was right to begin their cull of the Pilgrims' leaders. One by one they were summoned to London to answer questions. None felt able to refuse their king's command because to do so would have been treason, and in any case most of them felt secure in the pardon they had received. When they arrived in London they were arrested to await trial. By early May the 15 best known Pilgrims, including Lord Darcy and Robert Aske, were in Henry's hands. But the king was not to be satisfied merely with a sequence of judicial murders: he intended to squeeze every ounce of advantage out of the situation, and to be seen to be totally in control. It was decided that, although those arrested would be tried in London, they should also be indicted in Yorkshire. Indictment was a legal procedure by which a jury decided that there was enough evidence for the accused to be tried. The aim was to force the accuseds' friends and relations either to condone the king's actions or to be seen to be disloyal. The procedure, devised in general terms by Cromwell, sanctioned by Henry and implemented in detail by Norfolk, was heartless in the extreme. Two juries were to be established to decide on two identically worded indictments. Norfolk described his intentions in a letter to Cromwell.

1 My good lord, I will not spare to put the best friends these men
   have upon one of the inquests, to prove their affections whether
   they will rather serve his majesty truly and frankly in this matter,
   or else to favour their friends. And if they will not find then they
5 may have thanks according to their cankered hearts. And, as for
   the other inquest, I will appoint such that I shall no more doubt
   than of myself.

To nobody's surprise, both juries decided that all the accused should stand trial, as they quickly did. The claim was that they were being tried for actions taken outside of the period covered by the pardon, but, in the cases of Darcy and Aske in particular, there was no doubt that they were being judged for crimes which had already been pardoned. Nevertheless, all the accused were found guilty of treason. Most were executed in London, but Aske and several others were taken north for the sentences to be carried out where they would best illustrate the king's total control of the situation. The former Pilgrims made no attempt to save their erstwhile leaders. Norfolk had done his work well.

6 The Causes of the Pilgrimage of Grace

Henry claimed that the Pilgrimage of Grace had been caused merely by the false rumours that were in general circulation at the time, but no historian has taken him seriously. It is universally recognised that the king was conducting a calculated campaign of misinformation aimed both at assuring foreign governments that his problems were the result of misunderstandings that would easily be resolved (and that his régime was therefore in no real danger) and at providing individual Pilgrims with a good excuse to abandon their cause. This, of course, is not to doubt that the rumours existed and that they were instrumental in stirring up the commons to even greater fear and indignation than they already felt, but it is to maintain that the Pilgrimage would have happened even had the rumours not existed.

What were these rumours? Three rumours were most frequently reported to the Council by the JPs who sent in accounts of the early stages of the revolt. Most common was the belief that the king was about to order all parish churches to surrender their silver ware (normally a cross that was carried in procession and a chalice and a plate used in the Mass), and that tin ones were to be issued in their place. Although there is no evidence that the government ever contemplated doing this, it was perfectly believable that it might. After all, the property of the smaller monasteries was in the process of being seized with no compensation being given. The other rumours were reported in various forms. One was that the king was going to levy taxes on the various rights of passage (baptism, marriage and burial), thereby imposing considerable additional hardship on the bulk of the population who were already feeling economically hard-pressed. The second was that a law was about to be passed making it illegal for the choicer types of food (such as white meat) to be eaten by anybody below the rank of gentleman. The assumption was that this was a move both to keep the commons 'in their place' and to ensure that the well-to-do did not suffer in times of food shortage. Given the fact that it was already the case that only the rich were allowed to wear certain types of clothes, it was perfectly reasonable to believe that such discriminatory laws might be about to be extended.

The Dodds were very certain that they had identified the cause of the uprising. They asserted that it was a reaction against the religious changes of the previous five years, and that the discontent had been brought to the boil by the dissolution of the smaller monasteries, of which there were more than 100 in Lincolnshire and Yorkshire alone. While they recognised that only a minority of Pilgrims felt strongly about the restoration of papal supremacy in the Church, they argued that the official support given to the spread of reformist ideas, (typified by the appointment of a number of their leading supporters, such as Thomas Cranmer who had been the Archbishop of Canterbury since 1532, to senior positions in the Church), had caused massive resentment. Many people felt that the basic beliefs they had held since their childhood were being undermined, and they wanted those responsible for this to be punished. The balance of the available evidence supports this interpretation, and there can be no doubt that the majority of Pilgrims acted as if they were primarily motivated by religious factors.

However, many of the historians who have researched the period in the decades since the Dodds' work was carried out have wondered whether there might not have been more significant, although less apparent, causes of the revolt. One extensively explored suspicion has been that economic discontent lay behind the Pilgrimage. Strong support for this view is provided by events in Cumberland and Westmorland, where the commons seem to have been most aggrieved about the way in which their landlords had been increasing rents and the size of one-off payments, such as the entry fine which was paid when a new tenant took over a piece of land. But, with the exception of events in the north-west, it has proved impossible to build a convincing case to support the argument that economic factors were a prime cause of the uprising. It is obvious that there was a widespread discontent about a number of economic ills, but there is every likelihood that the Pilgrimage would have taken place even had this not been the case. So, the most that can be claimed for economic factors is that they seem to have contributed to the general discontent of the commons, making them more liable to revolt than they otherwise would have been.

Some historians have approached the issue of the causation of the Pilgrimage of Grace by posing themselves the question 'Whose revolt was it?'. Their reasoning has been that if the prime movers of the uprising can be identified, the motivations of that group will provide the most significant evidence of causes. Whereas the Dodds described the Pilgrimage as a revolt of the commons with gentry support, the current orthodoxy is that it was a gentry rebellion which was assisted by the lower orders. Thus, in recent decades, historians have tended to concentrate their attention on the motives of the well-to-do Pilgrims. The most convincing (though not totally so) explanation has been that the gentry deeply resented the fact that 'feudal' ways of doing things were being replaced by 'modern' approaches. The argument is that, although these changes had been underway for decades, they had gathered pace in the early 1530s when, under Cromwell's influence, the central government had become ever more interventionist. It is claimed that the northern gentry, in particular, believed that their traditional way of life, which was based on an acceptance of customary behaviours and beliefs, was being destroyed by the new ideas and the new men (that is, not from the traditional aristocracy) apparently favoured by the king. Thus, change in religion was viewed as just one component, although an important one, of a general malaise which affected all aspects of public life, making the Pilgrimage as much a social and political as a religious revolt.

In 1980 Sir Geoffrey Elton suggested that the prime movers in the revolt were the out-of-favour conservative court party, rather than the gentry. His contention was that they had despaired of being able to regain the upper hand from the 'liberals' (who had survived the disgrace of Anne Boleyn in early 1536 with their influence virtually intact) except by violent means, and were therefore reduced to the extreme course of armed rebellion. He very skilfully showed that the intention to revolt existed among many of the leading 'conservatives', including Lord Darcy, but he was not able to argue convincingly that they either masterminded or subsequently gained control of the Pilgrimage. The impression remains that, although the role of the opposition faction at court has traditionally been overlooked, the uprising was assisted by, rather than dominated by, those who resented their loss of personal influence with the king. The acid test seems to be, 'Would the Pilgrimage have taken place, essentially in the form it did, if the conservative court faction had not existed?' The answer has to be 'Yes'.

So, if one accepts the contention that the uprising was essentially a revolt of the gentry, willingly assisted by their dependants among the commons, the argument that the long-term causes of the Pilgrimage are to be found in the decline of feudalism, while the short-term causes revolve around the religious changes of the 1530s, is attractive. However, it must be remembered that any attempt to identify the causes of a movement involving tens of thousands of people must be tentative in the extreme. The evidence available is always likely to be partial and the suspicion remains that there were probably almost as many reasons for rebellion as there were rebels. Yet the effort is worth making, as long as the provisional nature of any conclusion is firmly borne in mind.

7   The Significance of the Pilgrimage of Grace

Historians have dealt with the significance of the Pilgrimage of Grace by asking themselves questions such as, 'How serious a threat was it to Henry VIII?'. The king himself made a determined effort to persuade people that it was merely a little local difficulty and of no great significance. However, recent commentators have disagreed strongly with this assessment. The generally held view has been that not only was the Pilgrimage the greatest threat to a monarch's authority in sixteenth century England, but also that it might have resulted in Henry's deposition and replacement by his daughter, Mary.

This conclusion has been reached on the basis of both the relative military strengths of the king and the rebels, and the potential for foreign intervention. It is not merely that writers have judged that Henry would have been hard pressed to raise an army large and committed enough to defeat the Pilgrims, even as they were in late November 1536. It is also considered likely that, had the rebels ventured south, they would have been joined by large numbers of discontents from the districts through which they travelled, making the possibility of military defeat ever more remote. Certainly it was the king's fear and the fervent hope of some Pilgrims that the rebellion would receive succour from abroad. It was anticipated that the Pope would decide that the time was now right to declare Henry deposed and to call upon all good Catholics to play their part in carrying out the sentence. It was also expected that Charles V would send troops to assist the rebels and to punish Henry for the pro-French bias of his foreign policy in recent years. It is considered that, although Henry was saved partly by his own skilful handling of the situation, the real reason for his survival was the failure of his potential enemies to act decisively. Not only did the Pilgrims accept a disadvantageous peace when they were strong enough almost to dictate terms, but the Pope and the Emperor were too slow to recognise the size of the potential advantage to be gained from the situation.

Yet, of course, the fact remains that the rebellion achieved nothing directly. It has even been claimed that, by making a further rebellion very unlikely, the Pilgrimage strengthened Henry's hand and made it possible for him to continue with the policies that had sparked off the uprising. After all, the dissolution of the major monasteries in 1538 made the dissolutions of 1536 seem almost insignificant. However, the contention that the Pilgrimage of Grace hastened the demise of the way of life it was attempting to safeguard is a little harsh. Henry had proved time and time again that he was prepared to follow policies that were dear to him almost whatever the opposition, and it is unlikely that because his potential opponents had been defeated in 1536 he pursued more radical policies during the rest of his reign than he otherwise would have done. In fact, it is possible that the opposite was the case. Even while the Pilgrimage of Grace was taking place Henry instructed that heretics should be persecuted more vigorously, in an effort to show that he was not the 'liberal' in religious matters that conservative opponents suspected him of being, and there is evidence that the more cautious approach to changes in religious beliefs and practices that is observable in the final decade of his reign was a calculated attempt to quieten some of the opposition to change that the Pilgrimage had revealed. Certainly, there is good reason to consider that the Pilgrimage of Grace was more than one of the 'might have beens' of the sixteenth century: it probably had more effect on subsequent policy than Henry would have cared to admit.

Making notes on 'Henry VIII and the Control of his Subjects'

If you examine the diagram that serves as a summary of this chapter you will see that it concentrates on issues and situations as much as on events. This is because the aim of the chapter has been to help you to identify historical problems and to consider a variety of ways in which historians have tackled them, as well as to describe what happened.

Of course, this does not mean that you do not need to memorise the main outline of what took place. So it would certainly be worth your while to compile a skeleton date chart of the events described in sections 2 and 5, so that you will be able to use the information as necessary to substantiate the arguments you will wish to put forward in essays that you write on this topic.

However, the major part of your note making should be the recording of brief answers to the questions that accompany the headings below.

1. Introduction

    What was Henry VIII's view of the relationship between a king and his subjects? (See also the extract on page 81.)

    Which groups of his subjects normally supported this view? Why?

2. Henry VIII, the Nobility and the White Rose Party

What conclusions can be drawn about Henry VIII's personality and character from the way he dealt with the White Rose Party?
3. The Maintenance of Law and Order
   What were the normal arrangements for the maintenance of law and order throughout the country?
4. Henry's Loss of Popularity
   Why had Henry become so generally unpopular by 1536?
5. The Pilgrimage of Grace
   What can be deduced about Henry VIII's character from the way he dealt with the Pilgrims?
6. The Causes of the Pilgrimage of Grace
   Place the causes in rank order, with reasons given.
7. The Significance of the Pilgrimage of Grace
   Place the assessments of significance in rank order, with reasons given.

Answering essay questions on 'Henry VIII and the Control of his Subjects'

Most examiners consciously strive to set 'balanced' papers, containing a mixture of specific and general questions. The normal pattern is for the questions that define a limited subject area to be directly and straight-forwardly worded, while the wide-ranging questions are phrased in vaguer terms. The reason for this is that it is often thought to be sufficient of a test of a candidate's preparedness for the exam to demand detailed knowledge of a limited area without making the wording of the question difficult – while it is thought reasonable that candidates who choose to show that they know 'a little about a lot' should be expected to handle questions that are less immediately accessible. Study the following questions.
   1. What were the causes of the Pilgrimage of Grace? Did it ever seriously endanger Henry VIII?
   2. How far is it correct to suggest that Henry VIII was a tyrant?
   3. 'Public disorder was never far below the surface.' Discuss with reference to early Tudor England.
   4. Why were Henry VII and Henry VIII so hostile to their own leading subjects?
   5. Was there ever a serious threat to Henry VIII's throne?
   Rearrange the questions in order of difficulty. Which do you think is the easiest? Be prepared to explain why you think this.
   Many people will have identified question 1 as the easiest – probably because it can be answered in a straightforward, descriptive manner. It is because such questions can be answered simply – at a low level – that

they are dangerous. It is very easy to know a lot about the subject, to write a long answer, but to score only about half marks. But it need not be so. Both parts of question 1 could be answered at a level that would attract high marks if they are interpreted challengingly enough, rather than by taking the easy way out! Both parts could be planned as a discussion, explaining the different points of view that historians have advanced, and concluding by suggesting which interpretations seem the more convincing. It would be good practice to attempt to plan such an answer to question 1.

Question 4 is also dangerous. Why is this? It is worth remembering that examiners are usually very impressed by candidates who can present an effective argument (backed up by evidence) that throws doubt on an assumption made in the wording of a question!

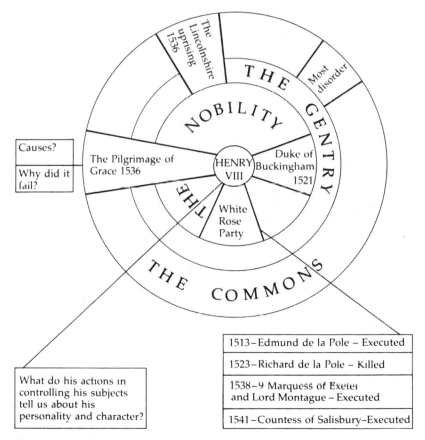

Summary – Henry VIII and the Control of his Subjects

Source-based questions on 'Henry VIII and the Control of his Subjects'

1 Henry's reply to the Lincolnshire Rebels, 1536
Carefully read the extract from Henry VIII's reply to the demands of the Lincolnshire rebels, given on page 81. Answer the following questions.
a) Paraphrase the argument that Henry put forward in the section between the two semi-colons ('and to take upon you ... to withstand;') (*5 marks*)
b) Identify three components of the tone of the extract, using a brief quotation to illustrate each one. (*3 marks*)
c) What can be deduced from the final phrase of the extract? (*2 marks*)

2 The Pilgrims' Oath, 1536
Carefully read the text of the oath administered to the followers of the Pilgrimage of Grace, given on page 82. Answer the following questions.
a) What is the significance of the reference to the 'king's person and his issue' (line 4)? (*3 marks*)
b) The oath contains mention of five demands. Identify them and in each case explain what lies behind the demand. (*15 marks*)
c) What can be deduced from the final phrase of the extract? (*2 marks*)

3 The Juries to hear the Pilgrims' Indictments at York, 1537
Carefully read the extract from the Duke of Norfolk's letter to Cromwell, given on page 87. Answer the following questions.
   a) Explain the meaning of the first sentence of the extract and comment on its implications. (*4 marks*)
b) Explain the meaning of the second sentence of the extract and comment on its implications. (*4 marks*)
c) Explain the meaning of the third sentence of the extract and comment on its implications. (*3 marks*)
d) Why could the strategy as described in the letter be considered to be foolproof? (*2 marks*)
e) Why was the Duke of Norfolk so determined to make a success of this episode? (*2 marks*)
f) What can be learned about EITHER Henry VIII OR Thomas Cromwell from the part he played in this affair? (*5 marks*)

CHAPTER 6

Thomas Cromwell

Before the 1950s almost all historians portrayed Thomas Cromwell as a
somewhat shadowy and unpleasant figure: as Henry VIII's unscrupulous hatchet man of the 1530s who received his just deserts in 1540
when he was abandoned and judicially murdered by his master. He was
normally presented as the ambitious go-getter who gained Henry's
favour by offering to make him the richest ruler in the world, and who
then went on to make good his promise by despoiling the Church in the
dissolution of the monasteries. It was argued that in order to control
public opposition to this campaign of state vandalism he erected a
ruthless system of repression that rested on spies and informers and
resulted in hundreds of innocent victims being executed for largely
imaginary crimes. He was thought of as being a thoroughly 'bad thing'.
This perception has been dramatically altered by one of the outstanding
British historians of the second half of the twentieth century. Sir
Geoffrey Elton has devoted the major part of a prodigious research
career spanning more than 40 years to a detailed investigation of the
central government of England in the 1530s, and in the process has
advanced a very different picture of the leading minister of the decade.
He has also made and maintained a case for the period being one of the
most important in the development of government in England – in fact
as being revolutionary. These claims have provoked an enormous
amount of historial debate and have stimulated large numbers of
researchers to undertake further work on the topic. As a result, the
1530s are possibly the most researched period in British history.
Although the focus of the debate has shifted somewhat over the decades
as the emphases of interpretations have been amended, the controversy
continues to provoke widespread interest and attention – as well as a
considerable amount of heat and animosity.

1 The Elton Thesis

Elton began by identifying what he termed 'a Tudor revolution in
government' as taking place between 1533 and 1540, while Cromwell
was Henry's chief minister. His main contention was that during these
years a series of changes were made (masterminded by Cromwell) that
in their totality marked the change from medieval to modern forms of
government. He went on to argue that, as this development was one of
the two or three major turning-points in the history of British politics, it
well deserved the title of revolution. His argument turned on his
definition of medieval and modern forms of government and his
assessment of what happened in the 1530s. He was quite specific about
the features that typified medieval government.

1 In every way, then, the great restoration of government after the
civil wars of the fifteenth century, the work of Edward IV and
Henry VII, represented the restoration of medieval government
at its most efficient. A financial administration based on the king's
5 chamber and the somewhat informal means adopted for audit and
control, the extended use of the signet [the king's private seal]
and the rise of the secretary, and government through individual
councillors rather than a council, all these marked the triumph of
household methods in administration.

He argued that modern forms of government were the antithesis of
medieval methods, in which administration was based on the monarch's
household. Modern systems of government were bureaucratic, being
based on properly constituted 'departments' that worked according to
agreed rules and procedures and which were therefore less open to the
influence of any one individual. The 'system' was paramount.

Elton maintained that in the 1530s sufficient changes took place in
the structure of government for the Henrician state to be considered to
have crossed the line that divides the medieval from the modern. He
identified two changes as being of particular significance. The first was
the replacement of a household system of finances, in which most of the
king's income was received by individual officers whose conduct was
not regulated by clearly formulated procedures and whose accounts
were not properly audited, by a bureaucratic system. In the new system
legally constituted departments received money from pre-specified
sources, paid out money for properly sanctioned reasons and were
efficiently audited to ensure that they were acting as they should. The
departments did not have titles that identified them as being financial
bodies. The Duchy of Lancaster was an existing 'department' that
administered the extensive lands and rights that had come to the crown
from the house of Lancaster, and it was the model for a number of new
'courts' which were established to administer most of the crown's other
sources of income. The most famous of these were the Court of First
Fruits and Tenths and the Court of Augmentations, set up to handle
the Church wealth that was newly coming to the king. They were called
courts because they also had the legal power to determine disputes over
what was owed to the government or what should be paid out by it. In
addition, the household was subjected to close regulation related to the
monies it still controlled so that it virtually became one of the new breed
of financial departments.

The second major change was the establishment of the Privy Council.
Elton argued that at some unidentifiable time in the 1530s (but
probably in 1536) the medieval system of a large council, with between
100–200 members, most of whom rarely attended, was replaced by a
Privy Council system in which a group of about 20 specifically
designated councillors assumed responsibility for the day-to-day run-

ning of the government. As the informality of the medieval system had normally resulted in one or two councillors (such as Cardinal Wolsey) gathering most power into their own hands, the change was seen as the movement of control away from a small number of influential individuals to a powerful bureaucratically-organised group.

Elton summarised his argument and placed it in a wider historical context by claiming

1 When an administration relying on the household was replaced by one based exclusively on bureaucratic departments and officers of state, a revolution took place in government. The principle then adopted was not in turn discarded until the much greater
5 administrative revolution of the nineteenth century, which not only destroyed survivals of the medieval system allowed to continue a meaningless existence for some 300 years, but also created an administration based on departments responsible to parliament – an administration in which the crown for the first
10 time ceased to hold the ultimate control.

* Although he spent a significant part of his time in the decades following the publication of *The Tudor Revolution in Government* in 1953 elucidating and defending his main thesis, Elton also found time to continue the investigation of Thomas Cromwell that his first researches had suggested might be fruitful. He had come to the conclusion that the traditional view of the minister was dramatically flawed, and he was anxious to prove his point. He wanted to replace the picture of the selfish and unscrupulous go-getter with one of an outstanding public servant who, although ambitious and willing to make unpopular decisions when he had to, was a great believer in the rule of law and was a dedicated reformer for the public good. He was sure that sufficient evidence existed for this to be done, as, when Cromwell was arrested in 1540, all his papers had been impounded and still remained available for the researcher to examine. The archive was very extensive. Cromwell had been a meticulously organised preserver of documents – perhaps the first Englishman to be so, and certainly in marked contrast to Wolsey. He had even retained the scraps of paper on which he jotted down *aide memoires* of the things to be done in the immediate future. All this was in addition to the many less complete collections of contemporary papers that existed elsewhere.

The final task to be undertaken was to debunk the tradition that Cromwell had acted as a brutal tyrant. This was effectively done in *Policy and Police*, published in 1972. The myth that Cromwell had established and maintained a network of paid spies and informers was exploded. It was clear that he had almost totally relied upon the normal channels of communication between witnesses to treasonable events, local members of the élite (especially JPs), and the Council in London, that had traditionally existed. Equally, the allegation that Cromwell had been responsible for securing the execution of large numbers of potential opponents based on inadequate evidence and by utilising questionable legal proceedings which went against all principles of natural justice was shown to be almost totally untrue. A detailed analysis of the cases of all those charged with treason during Cromwell's period of ascendency was carried out. Of the 883 people charged, only 329 (about 40 per cent) were actually executed. As over half of these followed the Pilgrimage of Grace, this was hardly evidence of a concerted reign of terror. More revealing still was the evidence that Cromwell was not only prepared to abide by the normal legal processes, but was frequently insistent that this should be done. As a result, many of the 60 per cent of unsuccessful prosecutions failed because of legal technicalities, which Cromwell readily accepted – although he was sometimes furious at those whose incompetence had resulted in cases being lost. The few examples that were found of him 'bending' the rules so as to secure convictions were cases in which Henry took a personal interest and over which he presumably made it clear to his minister that nothing less than a conviction would be acceptable.

However, Elton did not pretend that Cromwell had been all sweetness and light as he worked to maintain law and order. 'The king and his minister were not men of gentle kindness. They were riding a revolution [the Reformation] and they needed drastic instruments of repression.' There was no doubt that the powers with which they equipped themselves by act of parliament were extremely draconian. Not only was speaking out against the king as head of the Church punishable by death, but failure to report anybody who did so (known as misprison) was also treason and could result in imprisonment for life and the confiscation of all property. Yet, while Elton freely admitted that the general fear created by the existence of misprison could be construed as being almost a reign of terror in its own right, he stoutly maintained that Cromwell exercised his extensive powers with a general lightness of touch. He convincingly showed that the minister was quick to recognise that many of the supposed traitors who were reported to him were harmless cranks and posed no threat whatever. Some of these featured in reports over several years without action being taken against them. The other side of this coin was that he was quick to take action against those whom he felt could be influential with others. At least, Elton felt that this was a fair interpretation to place on the fact that about half of those prosecuted were clerics who, as a group, accounted for only 5 per cent of the population. So the impression was confirmed that Cromwell was an energetic hunter-down of possibly dangerous opposition. He kept this aspect of the government's work under his personal control, sending and receiving hundreds of letters every year on the subject of breaches of the peace, interviewing many of the suspected traitors himself, and deciding which cases to proceed with and which to abandon. But he was never bloodthirsty, taking lives almost for the fun of it. Those he acted against all seemed as if they were or could become the instigators of rebellious activity.

* The third branch of the Elton thesis was the attempt to establish Cromwell as one of the 'commonwealth' men. The commonwealth men were a collection of individuals who held similar views about the need for the government to take action to reform aspects of the country's social and economic life in the interests of the common good. They were not an organised group, but were actually part of a general western European movement of thinkers who advocated the novel idea that rulers could and should improve the lives of their subjects by introducing laws and regulations to maximise social harmony and to minimise selfish devisiveness. Before Elton's work, it was generally accepted by historians of the early modern period that such ideas were present but were of little practical effect in the England of the 1520s and 1530s, before blossoming briefly during the reign of Edward VI (1547–53). Elton's contention, most extensively spelled out in *Reform & Renewal: Thomas Cromwell and the Commonwealth* (1973), was that Cromwell built up a group of commonwealth men around him and used them to prepare programmes of legislation for him. These proposals formed the basis of a legislative programme which he attempted to implement, only to be frustrated by both the unwillingness of the commons to support him and by his fall which interrupted his efforts mid-term.

* When in future generations writers come to analyse what were the outstanding qualities that made Elton one of the remarkable historians of the twentieth century, they are likely to make mention of his facility both in dealing with obscure but significant points of detail and in charting the broad sweep of events. It is rare for a writer to be equally at home while discussing the implications of a scribbled note on the back of an otherwise unimportant document and in connecting events together in imaginative new ways so as to create an original perception of a period. But this is what Elton has managed to do during the decades of his intermittent work on Cromwell. In the process he has made many sweeping claims for the previously underrated leading minister of the 1530s. Not only was he 'the most successful radical instrument at any man's disposal in the sixteenth century', but he was even 'the most remarkable revolutionary in English history'. He was 'an administrator of genius' who displayed 'perspicacious dexterity in constructing afresh'. Because of the way in which he handled parliament during his period of ascendancy he was judged to be 'the country's first parliamentary statesman'. But perhaps the most significant claim was that Cromwell was 'a man who knew precisely where he was going and who nearly always achieved the end he had in view'. This was not intended to mean that Cromwell saw things in terms of personal goals; rather that he had a coherent vision of the revolution he wished to implement, that he was 'engaged on refashioning the very basis of the state'. This was Elton's overview statement into which all Cromwell's endeavours could be accommodated – his remodelling of the king's finances by bureaucratic procedures, his creation of the Privy Council as the body collectively responsible for executing the king's policies, his methods of containing opposition while the revolution took place, his attempts to introduce social and economic reform along the lines advocated by the commonwealth men, his establishment of the king in parliament as the highest authority in the state, and his destruction of the Church's position as a state within a state (see *Henry VIII and the Reformation in England* for a full discussion of this point).

2 The Debate

'I know there is a widespread feeling that the greatness of Thomas Cromwell is something manufactured for him long after his departure.' Elton's recognition (published in 1973) of his failure to persuade most commentators of the validity of his case was a misleadingly calm reference to a heated debate that had already featured strongly in historical publications for nearly 20 years and which, in fact, was to continue for many years longer. Both the extent and the intensity of the exchanges between the participants in what quickly became a wrangle were remarkable. Dozens of learned articles and sections in as many books have been devoted to arguing for or against the idea that the 1530s witnessed a wide-ranging revolution that was masterminded by Cromwell. At times the disputes have been so acrimonious and so personalised that many outsiders have been amazed by the attitudes and behaviour of those concerned. Such has been the emotional dimension of the debate, that John Guy (a historian worthy of respect in his own right) felt it necessary to assure the reader of his 'loyalty [to] and respect for' Elton before expressing doubts about aspects of his thesis. The choice of the word loyalty was particularly revealing.

In what ways, then, has the Elton thesis been attacked? Some critics have disputed the Elton thesis in general terms. The most telling of these overall attacks have been those that cast doubt on the claim that Cromwell was working to something like a master plan. It has been maintained that the coherence existed only in Elton's mind and that, although Cromwell at various times clearly held most of the attitudes and aspirations that have been attributed to him, they in no sense constituted a well-developed philosophy of government that he consistently attempted to put into practice. It has been argued that he was so easily deflected from his altruistic purposes by the political needs of the moment – especially the need to satisfy the demands of the king and to ward off attacks from political opponents – that he mostly acted as an opportunist rather than as the implementer of a grand design. The complaint has been that Elton was too quick to see a neat pattern of intentions and motives spanning the period 1533–40 when, in practice, none existed. This line of attack has been especially effectively pursued over the issue of Cromwell and the commonwealth men. It has been argued that the so-called group of advisers that Elton identified as existing in the later 1530s were actually a random collection of individuals who had approached Cromwell for patronage at different times, and that it would be equally possible to concoct 'groups' of advisers with a different point of view from among Cromwell's lengthy list of clients to whom he offered some financial support. While it is admitted that the numerous proposals for reform – many extensively annotated by the minister personally – existed among Cromwell's papers, it is argued that Elton failed to present a convincing case that there was ever a serious intention to introduce more than a tiny fraction of the measures. It has been maintained that Cromwell displayed a lively interest in the ideas of the commonwealth men and that he enjoyed discussing them, but that he was never really committed to them.

Besides arguing that Elton sometimes read into evidence conclusions that it would not support, various of the general critics have maintained that he miscalculated the significance of a number of the changes he described. The most striking example of this relates to the changes in the way in which the king's finances were administered. Whereas Elton categorised them as a move from the medieval to the modern, others have suggested that almost the opposite is the case. Their view is that the arrangements made by Cromwell represented a return to the type of system that operated in the high middle ages before the chamber system developed by Edward IV and Henry VII came into being. They therefore see what happened in the 1530s as a retrograde step rather than as pointing the way to the future.

Equally, several objections have been raised to Elton's assessment of the significance of the development of the Privy Council. Rather than judging it to be part of Cromwell's plan to revolutionise the government of the state, some have seen it as a move that was championed by his opponents as a way of limiting his power. Their argument is that the leading courtiers who resented Cromwell's dominance of events imagined that a properly constituted Privy Council system would ensure that they were involved in all important decisions, rather than being by-passed as they had tended to be during the previous few years. They claim that Cromwell did his best to limit the effectiveness of the new arrangements by keeping control of key activities (such as formulating agendas, writing minutes, and implementing Council decisions) in his own hands rather than passing them over to permanent officials who should have been employed to 'service' the Council. In particular, they draw attention to the fact that such officials were not even appointed until after the minister's fall, concluding from this that Cromwell conducted a very effective rearguard action to protect his freedom of manoeuvre. In addition, they recognise similar tactics as having been employed in developing the new system of financial administration. They more than suspect that a significant part of Cromwell's motivation for introducing the new arrangements was the desire to strengthen his hold on the government's finances. They lay particular stress on the way in which the bureaucratic processes of accountability were not applied to some departments until after 1540. In the meantime Cromwell was able to spend sizeable sums of the king's money as he thought most desirable and only on his own authority. This, it has been claimed, was hardly the way of working that one would expect from someone who was dedicated to introducing 'modern' methods of administration.

3 Assessment

Where, then, does the balance of advantage lie between Elton and those who have challenged aspects of his thesis?

The fact that no historian of note has been prepared to accept Elton's major findings suggests that the critics have had a very marked effect. This is so much so that it would be difficult to find a single scholar of repute who would agree that the main elements of the thesis remain intact. So does this mean that after all the 1530s were not a highly significant decade in English history? Most certainly not. Although Elton's thesis of a revolution in government masterminded by Cromwell is not acceptable in its original form, most historians agree that England in 1540 was a very different state from ten years previously. But most of the changes are seen as having been an integral part of the Reformation, and as such they are discussed fully in *Henry VIII and the Reformation in England*. However, it is appropriate to make mention of some important aspects of the transition within a consideration of the Elton thesis and the career of Thomas Cromwell.

Elton may have been investing Cromwell with greater single-mindedness and consistency than the evidence supports when he claimed that the minister possessed a clear vision of the state he wished England to become and that he set about creating it in a coherent manner. However, there is no doubt that Cromwell was to a large extent responsible for the consolidation and centralisation of the English state that took place during his period in office. The major change, of course, was the exclusion of papal authority from Henry's lands and the bringing together, in the person of the king, of the separate legal jurisdictions (temporal and spiritual) that had existed in England for half a millennium. Because this dramatic development was an integral part of the Reformation it will not be discussed in this volume. Yet it is important to remember that although this was the most significant element of the transformation of government and administration that took place in England during the 1530s, all the other developments were not dependent on it. For several decades there had been sporadic attempts to end the virtual autonomy of the numerous semi-independent franchises that existed within the king's territories. Thus Cromwell was in no way original in his policy of turning England into a state with a centralised and uniform system of administration. But he was unusual in both the extent and the success of his efforts.

His major successes were over Durham and Wales. Following the Norman Conquest in 1066, the County Palatine of Durham had been established under the jurisdiction of its bishop. Although the bishop owed considerably greater allegiance to the King of England than did the Prince-Bishops of Germany to the Holy Roman Emperor – he was, after all, directly appointed by him – those living within his diocese were immune both from all normal English legal processes and from government regulations. Thus the king's writ (legal powers) did not extend into the area and government policy was only implemented if the bishop chose to do so. It was, therefore, a significant step when, in 1536, Cromwell arranged for parliament to extinguish Durham's special status and privileges, and to legislate that it should be incorporated into the kingdom on the same basis as other counties. In the same year an even more extensive elimination of special status took place. By an act of parliament, which is often misleadingly referred to as the Act of Union – Wales and England had officially been combined since the thirteenth century – the whole of modern-day Wales and the portions of the English border counties that had previously been part of marcher lordships were declared to be an integral part of the kingdom in which the king's writ would fully run. Seven new counties were established and Shropshire, Herefordshire and Gloucestershire were considerably extended. The enforcement of English law in the Welsh counties was largely placed in the hands of the newly introduced system of JPs (bringing them into line with English practice) and the right to elect members of parliament was extended to them. A similar right was extended to Calais, which illustrated Henry and Cromwell's determination to incorporate this important continental base as fully as possible within the English state. The same was not done for the small group of islands just off the French coast that was also part of Henry's domain. Hence the Channel Islands – because they were thought to be politically and strategically insignificant – continued to enjoy the semi-independent status under the English crown that they retain to the present. Thus, with minor exceptions, Cromwell completed the process of transforming England and Wales into a unified nation state at a time when local rights in many parts of continental Europe had centuries of existence ahead of them.

At the same time steps were taken to ensure that Henry's control of some of the more distant portions of the country was increased. This was done by placing them under the control of regional Councils, whose members were appointed by the king, and whose responsibility it was to see that government policies were implemented in the localities. The existing Council of the North, based in York and with authority over Yorkshire, Durham, Northumberland, Cumberland and Westmorland, was transformed into an effective extension of the council in London, rather than being essentially a body to supervise the king's rights as a landowner in the northern counties. Even the problem of Devon and Cornwall, where there were thought to be insufficient major landowners of proven loyalty and dependability to give confidence that government policies would be enforced, was tackled by the establishment of a Council of the West. However, this proved to be neither popular nor effective and it was speedily abandoned once Cromwell had been removed from office. Although it is impossible to quantify the significance of these developments, it is almost certain that they removed some of the barriers to the creation of an ever strengthening sense of national identity in the decades to come.

4 Cromwell Re-assessed

Since Elton pioneered the radical re-evaluation of the life and career of Thomas Cromwell dozens of other researchers have made contributions that have fleshed out our understanding of this remarkable man. The result of all this endeavour has been the creation of as full a picture of a common-born Englishman who died more than four-and-a-half centuries ago as could realistically be expected. And it is a picture about which there is a surprisingly large degree of consensus among academic writers on the period.

For example, few would now dissent from the view that Cromwell was the best minister that any English monarch was fortunate enough to be served by in the sixteenth century. The force of 'best' is both that he was extremely good at the work he did and that he was dedicated to serving his master's interests. Wolsey, of course, was difficult to better in terms of application and political skill – although Cromwell may not have been far behind him in either of these respects – but his actions were so influenced by self-interest that Henry invariably paid a high price (always financial and sometimes political) for the service he received. With Cromwell there was no such problem. Among both contemporary commentators and modern researchers there is agreement that Cromwell's first thought was always how to achieve what his master wanted. On numerous occasions he abandoned a policy he favoured or reversed a decision already made if it became clear to him that this was not favoured by Henry. He seems never to have employed Wolsey's strategy of purposely misunderstanding an instruction in order to continue to pursue a cherished policy. However, it has often been suggested that Cromwell's loyalty to Henry was the result of his fear of the king rather than of a genuine devotion to his master. A contemporary visitor to court reported that:

1 the king beknaveth him twice a week and sometimes knocks him
   well about the pate; and yet when he has been well pummelled
   about the head and shaken up as it were a dog, he will come of the
   Great Chamber shaking off the bush with as merry a countenance
5 as though he might rule all the roost.

But this description should not be taken too readily at face value, as it
is suspected that the account is merely a repetition of a greatly
exaggerated story that was circulated by hostile courtiers who wished to
undermine the minister's authority. Yet it should be remembered that
there was often at least a germ of truth in even the most improbable
stories of the time that received widespread circulation among those
who were close to the events they described, and the account does fit in
well with what we know of both Henry's bullying tactics and Cromwell's proven willingness to put up with whatever was necessary to
retain the king's favour. Certainly it seems safe to conclude that
Cromwell did not manage to acquire a fraction of the room for
manoeuvre that Wolsey created for himself.

Cromwell and Wolsey were very similar in the qualities they brought
to the task of carrying out the king's business. They both possessed
minds of very high quality that were well able to formulate large-scale
plans and to evaluate the advantages and disadvantages of the options
that were open to them. Although Cromwell had received little formal
education, he had read extensively and had, for example, mastered
several languages by his own efforts. He possessed a powerful memory
– it is said that as a young man he memorised the entire New Testament
while riding across France on his way to Italy. Because he very much
enjoyed discussing problems and possibilities with other men of ability
his powers of reasoning were constantly enhanced, so that by the time
he rose to prominence he was generally recognised as being able to hold
his own with the most skilful advocates in the land, such as Sir Thomas
More. He was, therefore, regularly able to make the best possible
decisions based on whatever evidence was available to him. Both men
were also prodigious workers who not only devoted long hours to their
duties but who also transacted business at an unusually rapid rate. Thus
Cromwell was able to supervise most details of government personally
and to ensure that all decisions of significance received his careful
consideration before going to the king for final approval. This should
have allowed him to ensure great consistency of policy but this did not
happen. This was largely because he tried never to present to Henry a
proposal with which he was unlikely to agree. Hence he allowed himself
to be deflected from persisting with policies when he suspected that his
increasingly moody and changeable master was hostile to some part of
his intention.

5 Cromwell's Career

However, it should not be imagined that Cromwell was a meek and mild yes-man who was content to be a back-room boy merely carrying out the instructions that were handed down to him. What is known of his early life suggests that he was anything but a passive conformist. As is normal with those sixteenth century personalities who rose to prominence from obscure origins, little certain is known about him before he emerged onto the public stage. This is partly because most ordinary people of the time made no individual mark on the surviving records and partly because the new-men themselves were rarely eager to parade their backgrounds before their 'gentle' colleagues who generally regarded the low-born as little better than ex-slaves. In an era when exact age was of no significance, it is not even known when Cromwell was born, but it was probably about 1485. He was brought up in London in a family of modestly affluent artisans, but appears to have run away from home as a teenager, for reasons that cannot now even be reasonably guessed at. But his initiative and daring can be safely assumed because he crossed the Channel (a hazardous enterprise in itself) and made his way to Italy which was then the centre of European civilisation. It seems that his intention was to join the French army that was then attempting to regain the initiative in the long-running Italian wars. There is good evidence that he was present at a major French defeat, but it is unlikely that he was well-trained enough to have been anything but a camp follower.

Cromwell seems to have spent the next decade or so attached in a variety of capacities to members of the sizeable English community in Italy. He was obviously a young man with an eye to the 'main chance' because he learned enough about trading procedures to be employed in responsible positions by a number of merchants, who would normally have preferred to employ people who were either linked to them by blood or came recommended by a trusted commercial contact. As Cromwell possessed neither of these advantages he must have had outstanding personality and ability to advance his cause. When his patron of the moment, an English cardinal living in Rome, died in 1514 he decided to return to England. His offer of service was accepted by Wolsey, the then rising star, and he worked hard at the task of making himself valuable to his new master for several years before emerging as the chief minister's foremost legal adviser in the early 1520s. How he managed to acquire the necessary training and experience is not known, but it was probably a case of brilliance and determination making almost anything possible if he wanted it enough. Throughout the 1520s his enormous energy allowed him to do all that his master asked of him as well as building up a thriving private practice on his own account.

Cromwell revealed a great deal about himself by his reaction to Wolsey's sudden fall in 1529. He behaved in a very different manner from most of those around him. He neither became dispirited and inactive, assuming that the cardinal's leading followers would be disgraced along with their master, nor did he attempt to distance himself from the calamity by joining in the general vilification of the fallen idol. He summed up the situation rapidly and acted decisively by busying himself to secure his nomination to a currently vacant seat in the parliament that was about to gather at Westminster. His intention in doing so was two-fold. He wanted to advance his own claims to preferment by bringing himself to the attention of the king and whoever were to be the new leading figures at court. He also wished to be in a position to defend the interests of his former master. This display of loyalty to Wolsey during the cardinal's last months, as well as the skill with which he conducted the business involved in disentangling many of the fallen favourite's complex legal affairs, resulted in him coming favourably to the notice of Henry, who was soon very pleased to recruit him directly into his service.

Despite all the research that has taken place in recent decades, it has still not been possible accurately to chart the stages by which Wolsey's legal adviser became Henry's leading minister. There is just not sufficient evidence for it to be done. But however it happened, it was certainly not a rapid process, for it was not until the spring of 1533 that the major influence over the king was clearly his. Nevertheless, because it is known how the rise to prominence was not achieved, it is possible by a process of elimination to make informed guesses about the way in which it came about. Cromwell did not secure his promotion by successive appointment to a series of important state offices. In fact, at no point during the whole period of his ascendency did he acquire any of the major offices of state, and during the years in which he was manoeuvring himself into power all he managed to acquire was a selection of minor offices which brought him no more than a modest income and the opportunity to find out exactly how the existing administrative system worked (however badly) in practice.

Thus Cromwell's rise must have been by informal means, much as Wolsey's had been 20 years earlier. It is very likely that he won the king's favour by showing that he could think his way through problems and come up with solutions where his more senior (in terms of both experience and social status) could not. Of course, the seemingly insoluble problem of the time was how to bring the king's marriage to Catherine of Aragon to an end so that Anne Boleyn could become his second wife. It seems that Cromwell's emergence was the result of his ability to propose a realistic way forward and his possession of the administrative skills needed to put the policy into practice. These events are fully discussed in *Henry VIII and the Reformation in England*.

However, Cromwell was a very shrewd politician. He recognised that while his position relied entirely on the good opinion of his monarch, he was extremely vulnerable to the political in-fighting with which the

Thomas Cromwell

court was rife. One serious mistake, or even the appearance of one, could bring his official career to a premature close unless he had influential friends to protect him or a power-base from which he could mount an effective counter attack. There was little prospect of securing the former, as Wolsey, his long-standing patron, had recently died in disgrace and he had no relatives in high places to whom he could attach himself. He did make attempts to win the favour of the rapidly emerging Boleyn faction, but it was not surprising that his approaches were not warmly welcomed by a group that was deeply suspicious of anybody who had been connected with the cardinal, and which in any case wanted followers rather than additional leaders. So Cromwell set about the task of establishing a stronger position for himself. Although there is no direct evidence to indicate that this was so, it seems likely that he was the first person to recognise the massive potential of the minor post of Principal Secretary to the king, which was at the time little more than a highly confidential clerical position. Certainly he seems to have worked very hard to obtain his own appointment to the post. At first he substituted on a voluntary basis for the existing secretary who was on business for the king abroad, and he then elbowed aside others who aspired to the position and prevailed upon Henry to dismiss the current incumbent and to appoint him in his place. As the appointment depended entirely on a word of mouth instruction from the king – there was no documentary evidence to confirm what had happened – there can be no certainty about when this took place, but the most probable date is April 1534.

Cromwell utilised his position at the centre of affairs, with so much information and so many instructions literally passing through his hands, to create a situation in which anybody who wanted a favour from the king or who wanted something to be done was more likely to be successful if he gained the Principal Secretary's support first. Although he was never able to secure a stranglehold on the channels of royal patronage and decision-making of the type that Wolsey had established, he was able to build up a position in which hundreds of people depended on his good will for the furtherance or maintenance of their ambitions. This was especially the case in the years following the disgrace of the Boleyn faction in the spring of 1536, by which time he had secured the appointment of many of his own servants to key positions throughout the administration. Some sign of his increased dominance was his appointment as Lord Privy Seal in July 1536 which meant that a large majority of the king's most legally binding instructions only took effect once he had endorsed them. But the significance of the change should not be exaggerated. Most people had already become used to accepting that when Cromwell wrote or said 'His Majesty wishes that', the communication was virtually a royal command. Elton long ago showed in detail the extent to which Cromwell's word had become administrative law within the government.

 * In June 1540 Cromwell was arrested and charged with treason. He was executed the next month. Some historians have expressed surprise and even revulsion that this should have happened. However, given the relative insecurity of the minister's position, despite his best efforts to make it otherwise, and the increasingly fickle nature of a master whose limited constancy was frequently undermined by lengthy bouts of excruciating pain and their accompanying anger and frustration, it was almost certain to happen at some stage. The question for the historian to answer is not why the blow was struck but why it happened when it did.

Despite the fact that it was not proved possible to disentangle all the plotting and counter-plotting that took place, it is certain that events reached their climax very speedily. While it is true that Cromwell's position had been less strong since he began his espousal of the disastrous marriage to Anne of Cleves (see page 3) in 1539, he had subsequently been successful in recovering much of the lost ground. It was, for instance, a mark of very special favour, when a few months before his fall, Henry had created him Earl of Essex – a very rare elevation to the senior peerage of a man who had not even been born into a family with noble connections. This would certainly not have been done had Henry at that stage had even the remotest intention of cutting down his leading minister.

It seems as if the most influential of Cromwell's opponents – the re-formed Boleyn faction led by the Duke of Norfolk – had been able to produce a trump card that the new earl could do nothing to counter. They dangled before Henry a second niece of Norfolk's (Anne Boleyn had been the first) and mixed poison about the minister with the cup of sweetness about the 19-year-old Catherine Howard. The king was beguiled and agreed to believe the lies and misrepresentations about Cromwell as the price to be paid for securing the vivacious young woman who was to become his fifth wife. The grounds on which Cromwell was charged are not to be taken too seriously by searchers after the truth: first the decision was made to destroy him, then suitable grounds were sought. The charge most likely to impress Henry was that Cromwell had secretly been plotting to introduce a fully-blown version of protestantism, of the Anabaptist type, in the face of the king's known aversion to radical changes in the theology of his church.

There was sufficient evidence of Cromwell's personal sympathy for protestant beliefs for such a charge to seem credible – except that there could be little doubt that he was genuine in his frequently repeated assertions over the years that he would do or believe whatever the king instructed him to. To execute such an obedient servant for treason defied all logic, a realisation that Henry rapidly came to once his infatuation for his new wife-toy had rapidly run its course. Among the most striking ironies of a most bizarre episode were the almost simultaneous execution of Cromwell and the marriage of Henry and

Catherine (emphasising the impression that they were mutually dependent events), and the recognition by Henry that Cromwell's enemies had duped him as he unwillingly became convinced that not only had Catherine been free with her favours before her marriage, but that she had also regularly contemplated committing adultery once the reality of marriage to a physically repellant man about 30 years her senior had become clear to her. But there was little that the king could do to exorcise his remorse, except to consign Catherine and her closest associates to the same fate that had so unjustly befallen Thomas Cromwell. That, of course, could not bring back to life the only man who might have guided England successfully through the turbulent later years of Henry's reign.

6 Conclusion

So what, after all the research, debate, attacks and defences, can be accepted with a fair degree of confidence as the truth about the political career and historical significance of Thomas Cromwell?

A greater degree of consensus has emerged among historians than might seem likely, given the long-running disputes that have taken place. There is, of course, general agreement that Cromwell was a remarkably talented government official who exercised his outstanding abilities in turning Henry VIII's sometimes hazy political aspirations into fully worked-out policies that he then implemented in detail against considerable odds. This was possible because he was always able to keep the overall aim clearly in his mind while submerging himself as necessary in laborious work on even the smallest detail. In this way he was always able to distinguish between the vital and the trivial and to prevent himself from becoming bogged down in a morass of urgent but non-essential business. His work rate was phenomenal and made it unnecessary for him ever to develop the ability to delegate effectively. Comparisons across centuries are always controversial because of the major differences in available knowledge and techniques that applied, but several historians have been prepared to contend that Cromwell was possibly the most effective government minister of all time. Certainly nobody has argued convincingly that he was not.

If one accepts that Elton's grander claims for Cromwell's historical significance are interesting rather than convincing – and there is now little reason to avoid doing so – a large measure of agreement exists about the place of the 1530s in the long-term development of the English state. It was a decade during which the de-centralised and ill-defined medieval monarchy took on many of the features of the modern centralised, bureaucratic state in which the supremacy of national law began its long journey towards unquestioning acceptance. Most historians would now agree that although Cromwell held quite well-developed views on the desirability of this happening, the deci-

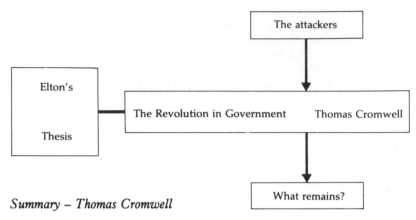

Summary – Thomas Cromwell

sions that led to changes taking place were piecemeal, were largely inspired by the king and were generally aimed at achieving other objectives. So it seems that a series of coincidences made it appear that a coherent policy was being pursued, when in fact the pattern that is normal in a complex organisation with networks of competing power groups was taking place. Decisions were being made under the pressures of the moment, with long-term aims providing only a framework within which the relative merits of the most readily available options could be assessed. Whatever may or may not have been Cromwell's hope of creating a new type of state, his prime motivation was always how to please his master in whatever was his mood of the moment. The miracle was that so much consistency of policy was achieved in such circumstances.

Making notes on 'Thomas Cromwell'

It is important to remember that your reading about Thomas Cromwell has not yet been completed. Although this chapter provides an examination of all the major issues about him that you will need to consider, it does not provide you with all the facts you will need to use when you discuss his historical significance 'in the round'. For that you will need to know much more about the part of the English Reformation that took place in the 1530s.

There are two important tasks for you to carry out following your reading of this chapter. You need to make outline notes on two sets of issues:

1. The Elton Controversy:
    What were the salient points of Elton's case?
    What are the main lines of criticism that have been levelled at his thesis?

What is the current 'state of play' in the controversy?
2. Thomas Cromwell
What is generally agreed about his contribution as Henry VIII's leading minister?
Over what about him do historians still disagree?
You will probably find it beneficial to attempt to answer the five questions directly.

Source-based questions on 'Thomas Cromwell'

1 The Elton Thesis
Carefully read the extracts from Elton's writings on pages 96 and 97. Answer the following questions.
a) What did Elton describe as being the single main element of medieval government as restored by Edward IV and Henry VII? What were the five component parts of this? (*6 marks*)
b) In what ways have some historians disagreed with this part of Elton's analysis? (*2 marks*)
c) What, in the second extract, did Elton claim to be the most important aspect of the revolution in government that took place in the 1530s? (*2 marks*)
d) In what ways have some historians disagreed with this part of Elton's analysis? (*5 marks*)

2 The Portraits of Wolsey and Cromwell
Carefully study the portraits of Cardinal Wolsey and Thomas Cromwell reproduced on pages 51 and 108. Answer the following questions.
a) Assuming that the pictures were to their subjects' liking, what can be deduced about the way in which each of the men wished to be portrayed? Specifically draw attention to similarities and differences. (*10 marks*)
b) What is the significance of the items resting on the table in Cromwell's portrait? (*5 marks*)

CHAPTER 7

The Final Stage

1 Introduction

Henry VIII died on 28 January 1547. It was not a sudden event. He had been seriously ill on and off for a decade and many had been the time when both his doctors and his court had expected that their patient and monarch would soon be dead. He was, after all, no longer young. The fact that he survived into his fifty-fourth year meant that he had already outlived many of his contemporaries in a period when a person at 40 was thought to be entering old age rather than middle age. And he was not a well man for his years. He suffered from excruciatingly painful swelling of his legs (some writers maintain that the evidence suggests that only one leg was affected) which periodically broke out into horrible sores, the discharging of which, paradoxically, brought him considerable relief. He was massively overweight, with a waist of over 50 inches, and other parts in proportion. This huge bulk seems to have increased the severity of the pain that he would, in any case, have suffered.

There has been considerable debate about the probable nature of his illness. For centuries it was assumed that he was experiencing the advanced stages of syphilis. The affliction was colloquially known in England as the pox or as the French disease, and in every other European state by the name of a despised or hated neighbouring country. To the Spaniards it was the English disease. Doctors incorrectly believed that if sufferers took small amounts of mercury the progress of the illness could be slowed down or halted, but there is clear evidence that Henry was not prescribed this treatment. So, at the time, it was not thought that he was a victim of the pox, and there is no evidence to support the contention that his physicians missed what would have been an obvious diagnosis. However, although there is general agreement about what he did not suffer from, no consensus has emerged as to what his illness actually was. The several books and many articles that have been written on the subject have all failed to win widespread acceptance, and it probably now has to be accepted that there is insufficient evidence for a fully convincing case ever to be made. But it does appear safe to conjecture that the king was suffering from more than one complaint, the major contenders being brain damage inflicted by a jousting accident in 1536 and vitamin deficiency resulting from an unbalanced diet. And, interesting though it is to speculate about the nature of his illnesses, it is their effect upon Henry that is of real historical significance.

The orthodox view used to be that the period from the fall of Cromwell to Henry's death was a time of steady decline in the affairs of

Henry VIII, painted by Cornelys Matsys in 1544

both the king and his country, with matters going from bad to worse, so that a desperate situation was left for his child-heir and his leading subjects to attempt to resolve. The last six years of his reign were typified as being a time of recurring crises which were largely caused by the over-reactions and growing eccentricities of an increasingly tyrannical and pain-maddened ruler. Henry was seen as oscillating between lengthy periods of black despair and depression and shorter interludes of unrealistic optimism, during the first of which times his decisions were likely to be so slow in emerging that their delay caused chaos in the affairs of state, and during the second of which rapid decisions were made based on totally unrealistic premises, and with equally disastrous results.

The expounders of this interpretation had at hand a picture that seemed to summarise their case. This was the portrait of Henry painted by Cornelys Matsys in 1544, (see page 115). Even though this was intended to be a flattering portrayal of its subject, it appeared to many twentieth century eyes to show the bloated face of a seriously sick man, whose meanness and even madness was apparent in the gaze of his piggy eyes and in the outline of his shrunken mouth. Here, undoubtedly, was a man about whom the widely circulating stories of power-crazed cruelty could be believed. And the hard evidence of the major affairs of state seemingly corroborated the case.

2 Catherine Howard

It is widely agreed that Henry's abortive fourth marriage, to Anne of Cleves, had been an error of judgement that must be laid at Thomas Cromwell's door, (see page 3). However, the king's fifth marriage, to Catherine Howard, which rapidly followed it, has generally been taken as clear evidence of Henry's flight from reality during the final years of his life.

Catherine was the daughter of the Duke of Norfolk's younger brother. She was but one of the dozens of the Howard clan's younger generation that was available for furthering the family's political and dynastic ambitions. The foremost of these was the Earl of Surrey, who was expected soon to assume the leadership of the family because his father, the Duke of Norfolk, was already in his seventies and could not be expected to live much longer. Surrey (or Norfolk as he would then be) would be second only to the royal family in terms of ancestral nobility, combining as he did the blood of the country's two premier families. Through his mother, the heiress of the last Duke of Buckingham (see page 52), he could claim descent from the Plantagenet kings, and from his father he inherited the mantle of the last of the élite Anglo-Norman baronage. Yet the family was not satisfied with this position. It wanted the high degree of political power that it thought had wrongfully been denied it by the Tudor kings. The first step was to remove the low-born servants who surrounded the king and who prevented the true nobles from occupying their rightful place in the affairs of state. In 1540 these upstarts were led by Thomas Cromwell. The plotting to remove him was elaborate. It seems that a minor element of their plan was to ensnare Henry in a romantic affair with a younger member of their family who would then be able to play a part in feeding the king with misinformation about his leading minister. It is unclear when the idea developed of turning an affair into a marriage, which would of course yield an even greater dividend if the woman involved was capable of both providing the old king with more children (who would probably one day inherit the throne, given the frailty of Edward and the ease with which Mary and Elizabeth could be declared illegitimate), and beguiling the king with her youthful charms.

Catherine Howard, aged about 19 (exhaustive research by her leading biographer has failed to uncover even the year of her birth) and an infectious fun-lover, was chosen as the bait. The first part of the plan could hardly have worked more successfully. Although it is unlikely that the prospect of winning her favours was an important factor in the king's decision to rid himself of Cromwell, Henry was certainly captivated by her almost as soon as she was introduced to court. She willingly became his mistress and, probably by pretending to be pregnant, was within a few months his wife. It would not have been difficult to explain away the loss of the putative baby, especially as there would be time for plenty more. The king was deliriously happy and enjoyed nothing more than showering his new queen with signs of his affection, whether they were jewels or political favours that she had been told by her mentors to ask of him. The Howard star was well and truly in the ascendant.

Unfortunately, for the long-term success of the venture, Catherine was as lacking in political sense as Anne Boleyn, the other niece of the Duke of Norfolk to become queen, had been blessed with a remarkable ability to handle the intrigues of Henrician court life. Catherine very quickly tired of pretending to love her husband as much as he adored her. With the stunning lack of political judgement that had typified Norfolk and the leading members of his family for decades, no effort was made to ensure that the queen behaved at all sensibly. In fact, she was actually encouraged in her dangerous behaviour. Her female 'minders' not only allowed her to find romantic (and probably sexual) satisfaction elsewhere, but they even undertook the arrangements that made it possible. They were right if they judged that the king was so besotted that he would not notice that his wife's attentions were not all being lavished on him. Henry suspected nothing. But the Howards' political rivals caught wind of what was afoot and triumphantly seized the opportunity to discredit their opponents. They gathered what evidence they could of Catherine's indiscretions and presented it to Henry. It was perhaps an indication of the way in which leading public figures feared their sovereign's wrath at this stage in his reign that the information was handed to him in a sealed document in the middle of a church service by the Archbishop of Canterbury, together with the whispered plea that he read it later and in private. As expected, Henry was infuriated by the contents of the paper, and speedily berated its authors for being hoodwinked by such obvious fabrications. But as confessions were painfully extracted from the young men involved, the king was left with no choice but to accept that his darling wife had indeed made a fool of him. The realisation that he had acted like a stupid and gullible old man over the whole affair sent him into a deep depression, and prevented him from exacting full vengeance from all those who had led him into this predicament. Although the queen, the female head of her household and the two men directly implicated in the extra-marital philandering were executed in February 1542, Norfolk and his close associates were allowed to hide themselves away from court in some disgrace but without punishment. Their triumph of 1540 thus became the eclipse of 1542, rather than the total disaster that might have been anticipated when first the scandal broke.

3 Foreign Policy

The centrepiece of the case against Henry's kingship in the 1540s has normally been the charge that his foreign policy was an enormous and costly failure, by which he squandered the wealth of the monasteries that should have made the monarchy financially independent of special taxes from its subjects for generations to come. It is maintained that he reverted to the discredited approaches of the first half of his reign, which he should have realised were likely to result in bankruptcy, while bringing neither him nor his country any compensating advantages. He stands accused of seeking to regain his lost youth, especially after the morale-shattering experience of Catherine Howard, by seeking military successes abroad when there was no realistic possibility of securing them. It is said that not only were his aims unrealistic, but that they were pursued with such incompetence that, even had the policies stood any chance of success, they would have been turned into disasters by the way in which they were implemented. The abiding images are of a leader sending his armies to conquer Scotland without himself either possessing a map of the country or having more than a very hazy and inaccurate notion of the geography of the lands north of Hadrian's Wall, and of a fat old king being winched onto his horse in full armour (with leg pieces cut away to accommodate grotesquely swollen limbs) when setting out to head his troops on a continental campaign, while those who dared (allies and subjects alike) begged him to remain at home so that his royal person would not be risked in the uncertainties of combat.

There is considerable evidence to support this interpretation of events.

It had seemed in the 1530s that Henry had learned the pointlessness of pursuing a 'forward' foreign policy. Possibly under the influence of Thomas Cromwell, he had left the continental super-powers (France and the Habsburg empire) to carry on their debilitating rivalry while he concentrated his attention on affairs at home. He had even managed to steer clear of major trouble during the hazardous years of 1538 to 1541 when it had seemed that a grand coalition might be formed against him. At times during these years England's international position had appeared potentially disastrous, with the Pope leading the way by declaring Henry a heretic who should be deposed, and the Scots seeming eager to join with Charles V and Francis I, who reputedly had made peace with one another so that they could combine their forces in order to carry out the Pope's bidding. It was all the more amazing, therefore, that Henry should have sought to go to war once these hazards had been survived and when a renewal of hostilities between Charles and Francis in 1542 had seemed to indicate that England was now properly in the clear. But this is just what he did.

His major aim seems to have been to win a significant victory against the French. It appears that his intention was thereby to increase his 'honour'. He may have harboured hopes of a victory that would have resulted in a major acquisition of territory in northern France, but it seems more likely that he would have been satisfied with a very limited gain, as long as it was recognised by his fellow rulers as significant. But he was well aware that any attack on France must be preceded by action to remove the threat of an invasion from Scotland while his armies were on the other side of the Channel. The centuries' old *entente* between France and Scotland that was primarily aimed at England was obviously as strong as ever. Under the leadership of Henry's nephew, James V, Scotland had shown itself keen to join in any co-ordinated attack on 'the old enemy' that might have been mounted in 1539 or 1540.

a) Scotland

Henry had a low opinion of the courage and the perseverance of his northern neighbours. He imagined that they could easily be frightened into quiescence. He summoned James V to meet him at York in the summer of 1541 during his one and only 'progress' north of the home counties, so that he could bully his nephew into abandoning his friendship with England's potential enemies on the continent. Henry was genuinely surprised that he was forced to wait in his northern capital in vain while the King of Scotland issued a stream of implausible reasons why it was imperative for him to remain within his own kingdom. When further diplomatic pressure was met with responses that proved the Scottish king was merely playing for time by fobbing off his uncle with fine words of little precise meaning, Henry decided that it was time for a show of force. In the summer of 1542 an army led by the Duke of Norfolk was sent to overawe the Scots by looting and burning enough towns and villages to warn them that worse might follow unless they displayed a proper sense of deference to English interests in their dealings with other states. But, although the armed raid did an amount of damage, it was so poorly organised and provisioned that it was forced to return south much sooner than had been planned. Thus James was persuaded of England's weakness rather than of her strength, as had been Henry's intention. He was therefore emboldened to launch his own punitive raid south to show that he was not in the least overawed by his stronger neighbour.

The result was the battle of Solway Moss in November 1542, which was one of Scotland's greatest military humiliations. And to make matters worse, it was largely self-inflicted. A large and well equipped Scottish army trapped itself in a bog when confronted by a small and ineffectual English force. It was paralysed by bitter rivalries between its component parts, which meant that no leader would take orders from any other. Much of the army chose to surrender rather than to fight, while the remainder fled. A muddy grave awaited many of those in flight, and the English troops were presented with more nobles and gentlemen as captives than any army of its quality had ever acquired. The Scottish army had ceased to exist through a sequence of incompetent actions that were almost unparalleled in the annals of war. James V had been in Edinburgh at the time, but when he died a fortnight later, it was not surprisingly rumoured that it had been of shame. He left as his heir a baby daughter who had been born only a few days earlier.

The news of these events caused Henry to reassess his policy. His aspirations quickly changed from keeping Scotland quiet to seizing control of the country. Perhaps he knew what had happened when the Duke of Brittany had died in similar circumstances in the 1490s. Then, wardship rights over the young heiress had been claimed on behalf of her nominal overlord, the King of France, who was himself a child. She had subsequently been married to her guardian, and France had thereby acquired a large new province for itself. Kings of England had long claimed to be the overlords of the Kings of Scotland and, although this claim had nearly always been successfully resisted, Henry now set about attempting to do to Scotland what France had done to Brittany. But rather than marching an army into his intended acquisition in order to capture the child he claimed as ward, as the French had done, Henry attempted to achieve his ends by peaceful means. Presumably he did not want to divert his resources from the invasion of France that he had already secretly decided to undertake.

However, success in his Scottish policy was to keep eluding Henry. It was this inability to clinch victory when he seemed to hold the overwhelmingly strong hand that has led many historians to castigate him for gross ineptitude. It can be argued that at every stage he made the wrong decision. He loaded the nobles captured at Solway Moss with presents and returned them home on their promise to do everything possible to advance the English cause. They did nothing of any consequence. Months were wasted in negotiating a treaty (the Treaty of Greenwich of July 1543) with Scottish representatives which, in any case, failed to secure either of England's main demands. Mary, James V's infant daughter, was to remain in Scotland until the age of ten, and was only then to be brought south to be prepared to marry Edward, Henry's son and heir. The English requirement was that she should be handed over straight away so that there would be no room for subsequent double-dealing. In addition, the Scots were allowed to maintain all their existing treaty obligations to France. While these negotiations were being dragged out, Scotland's military capability was being rebuilt. At the end of the year the Scots declined to ratify the treaty, which therefore became a dead letter. Efforts were made to buy the support of the leading Scottish political figures, but although the gold was normally accepted, value for money was never received. In early 1544 it was belatedly realised by Henry that a show of force would again be necessary if the Scots were to do as the English required. But the lightning ten-day campaign that resulted in the burning of Edinburgh was so obviously the wrong option. Scottish disunity was thereby banished and both the country's ability to put an army in the field and to provide safe havens for the receipt of French supporting troops were undiminished. By the time Henry died Scotland was more hostile to England than ever and had lost none of its ability to mount effective raids southwards at the most politically damaging moments. It would seemingly not be too harsh to classify Henry's treatment of Scotland in the 1540s as an abject failure. A winning position had been lost at very considerable expense and stalemate was now the best that could be aspired to for the foreseeable future.

b) France

There can be no doubt that during the last six years of his life Henry was much more interested in his dealings with France than in those with Scotland, which were rarely viewed as more than a means to an end. As early as the summer of 1541, when he was still basking in the imagined warmth of Catherine Howard's love, his mind was turning to the possibility of mounting a second expedition (following that of 1513) to seek glory in France. It was probably the fact that he was being wooed by Charles V as a potential ally in the latest round of the Habsburg-Valois struggle that enabled Henry to escape in mid-1542 from under the black cloud that the treachery of his fifth wife had caused to settle over him. Although he worked hard in an attempt to force Charles to pay dearly for his support, he ended up agreeing in February 1543 to join the Emperor in an attack on France with nothing of substance to show for all his diplomatic efforts. Both parties agreed to lead a large army in person against the French in the following year, to co-ordinate a march on Paris, and not to make peace separately, but there was nothing to Henry's particular advantage in this.

It was something of a surprise (given the high failure rate of rulers to keep to their treaty obligations) that both allied armies took to the field at the agreed time in 1544. But there the effective co-operation of Charles and Henry ended. Henry used every excuse to avoid the commitment to head for Paris, and lost little time in marching most of his army from its base in Calais to lay siege to the port of Boulogne. It appears that he had always intended to make the capture of this relatively unimportant prize the cornerstone of his campaign. Charles also seems to have had private objectives of his own, although as his were pursued once it became clear what Henry's tactics were to be, his case that he was let down by his ally carries some weight. But he was not slow in settling the score. While the English forces made relatively short work of Boulogne's defences, the French limited themselves largely to diplomatic activity. And Charles was receptive to his enemy's advances. It was a poignant coincidence that on the very day that Boulogne surrendered to the English army (led by the Duke of Suffolk but with the king in attendance), Charles and Francis signed a treaty of peace. The French were now able to devote all their military attention to the invader from across the sea. But Henry had no intention of facing the full might of France alone. Boulogne was amply garrisoned and provisioned, and the king and the majority of his army returned home to celebrate their 'triumph'.

The season was now too advanced (little warfare took place in the autumn or winter) for the French to make more than a fairly nominal attempt to regain their lost territory. Their major effort to extract revenge would have to wait until the late spring of 1545. It soon became clear to Henry from the intelligence he received that the French were planning to give the English a taste of their own medicine by launching an invasion across the Channel. This news was acted on speedily in the southern counties, where the fortifications that had been erected during the war scare of five years previously were added to and the local musters were organised so that they could rapidly march to wherever the greatest danger threatened. English apprehension must have been considerable as the huge size of the French force that was being gathered became known – including a number of galleys being brought overland from the Mediterranean to the Normandy coast. But in the event the campaign of 1545 was a huge anti-climax. Francis, having no base on English soil corresponding to Calais from which to work, was forced to attempt to land his army directly into hostile territory. His decision was to aim his attack directly at the heart of the English naval defences at Portsmouth in the hope that his huge fleet would destroy its opposite number and would win him a relatively uncontested disembarkation. But the incompetence of his commanders was such that – hindered by adverse winds that kept blowing the French ships back towards their own coastline – the two fleets were not brought close enough to engage in battle before French supplies of food were exhausted and a retreat had to be ordered. The English had suffered serious damage to their finances (as had the French) but otherwise had escaped very lightly. A little destruction had been carried out by a small raiding party that had landed on the Isle of Wight and one of the prides of Henry's navy, the 'Mary Rose', had sunk itself in Portsmouth harbour by attempting to manoeuvre with its gun ports open. Even in his wildest dreams, the victor of Boulogne could not have expected to escape so lightly. An additional bonus was that Boulogne's defences held out against all attempts by the French to breach them. Military stalemate had been reached.

However, it soon appeared that diplomatic activity was to be as incapable as force of arms in bringing the war to a conclusion. The major stumbling block was that, whereas Francis was unprepared to sign a treaty that left England in possession of any territorial gains, Henry was not willing to hand back Boulogne so soon after its capture. But eventually a formula that satisfied both kings was devised. In June 1546 the Treaty of Ardres (a village very close to the site of the Field of Cloth of Gold) was signed. Francis was to regain all the territory, including Boulogne, that Henry had taken two years previously. Thus his honour was preserved. But the handover was not to take place for eight years, and was only to happen then if, in the meantime, large sums of money had been paid to the English. It was confidently expected in London that all the French gold would not be forthcoming, and that Boulogne would therefore remain in English hands indefinitely. Thus Henry's honour was also preserved.

Although it could be argued that the treaty was more to Henry's advantage than to Francis's, it is much easier to maintain that neither side benefited from either the war or the peace. Certainly, most historians have chosen to heap criticism on Henry for the entire French episode. It has been pointed out that the cost of the enterprise could never have been matched by the gains in either territory or prestige. It is even clear that the monies promised by Francis were insufficient to meet the enormous expense of defending Boulogne in the years before the handover was scheduled to take place, let alone reimbursing Henry for the initial cost of capturing the port, as was the theory of the settlement. The colossal financial irresponsibility of waging such an unnecessary war against France has amazed most commentators. It is not only the sheer expense (over £2 million, equivalent to a decade's normal government expenditure), but also, and mainly, the expedients to which Henry had to resort in order to raise the money that have been the subject of adverse comment. The heavy taxation and forced loans which yielded more than a third of the required amount brought immediate hardship to some members of the propertied classes, but was bearable. Less excusable was the way in which the future was mortgaged and confidence in the country's financial system was undermined. Thomas Cromwell had imagined that the acquisition of the monastic lands in the 1530s would guarantee the crown's financial independence for generations, and yet the king sold most of what remained (over £800,000 worth) in order to pay for the campaign of 1544. In addition, he borrowed about £100,000 on the foreign markets, a debt that his successors would have to repay. But possibly the least defensible of his actions were his devaluations of the currency. Twice he resorted to the fraudulent activity of calling in the country's silver coinage and re-issuing it with a lower content of precious metal but with the same face value. Although the operation provided him with more than a third of a million pounds in clear profit, it engendered such doubts about the future of the English currency that economic activity within the country slowed appreciably as those with capital adopted an increasingly 'no risks' strategy of spending rather than investing.

4 Henry the Tyrant

The case against Henry's conduct of foreign policy in the final stage of his reign is that he failed to achieve the successes that were available to him, while squandering his wealth and endangering the financial strength of his successors by attempting to win military glory on the continent. But an even more damning indictment has often been made of the way he ruled the country in the years before his death. He has been described as being a typical tyrannical bully who abused his authority by punishing not only those who dared to disagree with or to oppose him, but also many of those whom he only suspected of wishing to do so. He has been said to have operated a primitive reign of terror in which everybody spied on everybody else and in which fear of having one's words or actions misrepresented sapped initiative at all levels of government, as officials remained inactive unless they received specific instructions from an authorised superior. What is worse, it has been maintained that Henry took a perverted pleasure in watching his subjects squirm, for he let it be known that he was likely to forgive those who made a full confession of their faults and pleaded for his mercy. Sometimes he even set up situations seemingly for the sole purpose of causing maximum embarrassment to those who were attempting to carry out his instructions.

One of the incidents that has most often been recounted to illustrate these facets of Henry's kingship is the attempt made in 1546 to arrest Catherine Parr, his sixth wife, on suspicion of heresy. Henry had married Catherine presumably to bring him comfort rather than excitement (see page 4). He probably learned of her 'advanced' religious views after she had become his wife. The 'conservative' faction at court (of which the Duke of Norfolk was a leading member) attempted to do to Catherine Parr what the 'progressives' had previously done to Catherine Howard. But this time the charges were based on religious rather than sexual misconduct. There was unambiguous evidence that in her beliefs and practices Queen Catherine was closer to the Protestants than she was allowed to be by law at the time. Wriothesley, the lord chancellor, was chosen by his colleagues to present the evidence to the king. He must have done his work well because Henry agreed that his wife should be arrested and taken to the Tower for questioning. It seems that he then ensured that Catherine was told about what had been arranged, because within hours she had sought her husband's presence and had won him over by her promises that she would believe and do whatever he, in his superior wisdom, instructed her to. Henry pronounced himself satisfied that all was well but, presumably on purpose, 'forgot' to tell Wriothesley that the situation had changed. When the lord chancellor duly appeared the following afternoon with a contingent of guards to arrest the queen, he was treated to a torrent of abuse from the king for daring to attempt such a stupid and possibly treasonable act. Henry had well and truly displayed the fullness of his power.

A similar incident had previously occurred with Archbishop Cranmer whom the 'conservatives' also accused of being a secret Protestant. On this occasion Henry took obvious pleasure in instructing Cranmer to investigate the charges himself. The accusers were thereby confronted with the prospect of being judged by the very person they hoped to discredit. It is little wonder that no evidence was found to be forthcoming! And Henry had shown that there was little point in attempting to attack the only one of his senior office holders whom he trusted completely. Cranmer had shown over more than a decade that he had no personal ambition and that he was prepared to do whatever his monarch required of him.

The Duke of Norfolk had established a somewhat similar reputation for subservience to his royal master. He had survived several highly dangerous situations – especially at the time of the disgraces of his nieces Anne Boleyn and Catherine Howard in 1536 and 1542 – by throwing himself totally on his sovereign's mercy and by proving that he would carry out whatever duties were assigned to him. But his good fortune appeared to have run out at the end of 1546 when he was implicated in the treason of his eldest son, the Earl of Surrey, who had unwisely hinted that his ancestry gave him as much right as anyone else to be a future king of England. Henry showed his paranoia about any possible challenge, however distant, to his dynasty, by having Surrey executed. It is thought that had the king lived for one more day, Norfolk would have shared his son's fate. As it was, a mixture of good fortune and timely subservience had allowed him to live long enough to see another reign.

* However, it has been Henry's desire to control events even from the grave that has provided historians with their most quoted evidence of the king as megalomaniac during his final years. The issues have been the contents and the timing of his last will and testament. There was never any doubt that Henry's successor would be his only son, Edward. But once it was recognised that it was highly likely that Edward would still be a minor when his father died, (he could not be declared 'of age' until the mid-1550s at the earliest), all interest at court centred on the arrangements to be made for the government of the realm in the years before the new king attained adult status. It was well understood that whichever faction secured the dominant position during Edward's minority would be able both to exercise enormous power and to acquire considerable wealth at the monarchy's expense.

The two contending factions, although they were anything but settled in their composition, were the 'conservatives', headed by the Duke of Norfolk, and the 'progressives', led by Edward Seymour, Earl of Hertford, who was Edward's dead mother's brother. The 'conservatives' have been so-called because they both favoured keeping the teachings and practices of the Church of England as traditional as possible and believed that the king should seek his advice from his leading nobles rather than from men of common birth as had tended to happen since 1485. The most politically able of their active members was Stephen Gardiner, the Bishop of Winchester, whose plottings had been behind most of the attempts to discredit individual 'progressives' ever since he had lost the struggle with Thomas Cromwell to win the king's favour in the early 1530s. The 'progressives' had been identified with Cromwell during his period of dominance. Since his fall in 1540, they had naturally been somewhat in disarray. Perhaps their obvious new leader would have been Thomas Cranmer, Archbishop of Canterbury, as he had long been known to be sympathetic to their leanings towards Protestantism in religion. But Cranmer was interested neither in politics nor in seeking greater power for himself. His competitive spirit was minimal. It was therefore left to Edward's relations on his mother's side to set about rebuilding the fortunes of the faction that favoured change.

The historians who have seen Henry as the villain of the piece claim that he was not only well aware of the struggle for power that was taking place around him, but that he actively encouraged it so that he could play off one group against the other, and thereby retain effective control himself. It is in this light that his final will and testament has most often been interpreted. In it Henry specified that the country should be ruled after his death by a Regency Council, whose members were named by him and who could not subsequently be changed. It was also stated that the Council's decisions must be corporate, with no member being given greater prominence than any other. This attempt to stop the emergence of a leader, together with the fact that the Council appeared to be composed of equal numbers of 'conservatives' and 'progressives', has resulted in the claim that Henry was trying to ensure that politics remained 'frozen' in their existing state until his son was old enough to decide for himself what changes, if any, were to be made.

The timing of both the drawing up and the signing of the will have also been used to support the case that Henry was a tyrant who used particularly unpleasant methods during the latter part of his reign. The evidence has generally been thought to show that the will was drafted towards the end of December 1546 but that it was not authorised to be signed until a month later, when the king knew that he was about to die. The explanation that has most often been given for this sequence of events has been that the existence of the unsigned will, of which those named in it were aware, was a ploy by Henry to intimidate his leading subjects further. The fact that the document was unsigned was a clear threat that if those named in it did not please him in every detail, the wording of the will would be altered to their disadvantage before it was made final.

Thus the traditional interpretation has been presented, with minor variations, over many years. Henry has been described in the final stage of his life – and up to within hours of his death – as a selfish and unscrupulous tyrant who stumbled incompetently from disaster to disaster, harming the interests of his office, his subjects and his country in the process. It has been maintained that he left behind him serious difficulties that his immediate successors barely survived, and then only with a modicum of good fortune. The implicit judgement has often been that it would have been better for the interests or the reputations of all concerned had he died somewhat earlier than he eventually did.

5 Other Interpretations

Although no serious attempt has been made to paint the final years of Henry VIII's reign as a period of either successful government or national benefit, numerous *caveats* have been made to the orthodox condemnation presented above. In total, they could not add up to a reversal of the traditional interpretation, but they could provide the basis of a significant reassessment that might judge Henry much less harshly. Mitigating evidence has been presented that could be used to soften each of the 'charges' against him.

a) Henry's Marriages

There is little that can be said in Henry's defence over his relationship with Catherine Howard, except that clearly he sinned less than he was sinned against. But he was undoubtedly gullible to imagine that the young woman presented to him 'by chance' at Stephen Gardiner's house was anything but a 'plant'. And he was unwisely trusting to believe that the appointment of one of the queen's former male friends to her royal household was as innocent as it was claimed to be. Yet, to his credit, he seems to have learned from his mistakes. When he came to choose another wife, he selected a woman who possessed the qualities that he really required, rather than the surface glitter that appealed to his vanity. Catherine Parr may not have been quite the frump that, as a twice married, childless, and seriously religious widow of 30, she has sometimes been made out to be, but she was undoubtedly solicitous of the welfare of her husband and her three step-children and did much to ease the suffering of her husband's final years. Henry was definitely at fault if judged by modern standards for wanting a wife who was willing to defer to him in every matter, but he was realistic in knowing what he wanted and in ensuring that he got it. For those who consider that it is only historically valid to judge people by the standards of their time, the sound judgement he displayed in making his sixth marriage should possibly be offset against the criticism that has justly been levelled at his action over his fifth.

b) Scotland

There can be little doubt that Henry was generally unsuccessful in his dealings with Scotland during the 1540s. The most that can be said in his favour is that his northern rivals did not utilise the fact that he was abroad in the summer of 1544, or the threat of a French invasion of southern England in 1545, as advantageous times to sally forth against their traditional enemy. And it should be remembered that the absence of a war on two fronts had been all that Henry had aspired to at the outset. However, it is dubious whether Scotland's lack of offensive military activity in 1544–5 was a result of English actions. It seems more likely that it was caused by the debilitating internal rivalries that followed the death of James V rather than by any destruction of Scotland's armed might by Henry (Solway Moss must be regarded as a self-inflicted wound), or by any fear of English reprisals.

Some attempt has been made to lessen the criticisms of Henry's actions once his aim became to gain control, rather than to neutralise Scotland, by contending that the historians who have blamed him for not launching a military attack northwards in order to seize the baby Mary immediately after the death of James V were unrealistic in their belief that such a venture would have been successful. There would have had to be massive incompetence on the part of the Scottish factions for an English raid to have been allowed to capture Mary. Yet this hardly constitutes a defence of Henry. Therefore, it seems that one is left with a choice of judging him to have been unsuccessful in that he squandered a winning position by a series of injudicious decisions, or that he was unsuccessful because his aims were unrealistic and beyond his power to achieve. Subsequent history suggests that the French assimilation of Brittany could not have been paralleled by similar action by England in Scotland.

c) France

A much stronger case can be made that Henry has traditionally been too severely criticised for his French policy in the 1540s. If one compares him with the two other contemporary western European rulers – Charles V and Francis I – who aspired to international recognition for their military feats, the conclusion can be reached that Henry did not perform relatively badly. Both of his competitors for fame could call on resources that were many times more extensive than those available to the King of England, yet their permanent achievements over 30 years amounted to very little indeed. And in the 1540s Henry was the only one to emerge with a recognised victory to his name. Even if the criterion used to judge is relative value for money, it can be claimed that whereas Charles and Francis spent much more than Henry, they clearly gained less, both in territory and in glory.

Even the criticism that Henry brought the English monarchy near to bankruptcy for very little purpose is severely weakened if one accepts that people in history should only be judged by their own values. Given Henry's beliefs about the nature of kingship and the importance of 'honour' (see page 18), not only was his declaration of war against France consistent with his principles, but the capture of Boulogne and the Treaty of Ardres were clear-cut victories for him. In such circumstances, the cost argument becomes irrelevant because according to Henry's standards the acquisition of glory was his main vocation, and it would have been unkingly to consider the consequences. So, depending on the point of view adopted by the observer, it is logically possible for an alternative interpretation of the war with France to that traditionally advanced to be argued successfully.

d) Henry and the Government of England

Research in recent decades has thrown the greatest doubt on the view of Henry as an aging tyrant. It is still generally accepted that this is how he thought of himself, and how he performed on well-publicised occasions. But what has been quite effectively challenged is the idea that this is how things were for most of the time between Cromwell's fall and the king's death. The traditional interpretation very much depends upon the validity of the claim that in the final stage of his reign Henry acted as his own chief minister, attending to the *minutiae* of government in much the same way as Wolsey and Cromwell had done in previous times. This allows it to be maintained that the king played the factions off one against the other – that he literally did divide and rule.

However, the evidence that has emerged as the period has been more extensively researched can be used to suggest that the factions manipulated the king at least as much as they were manipulated by him. The core of this alternative interpretation is that, although the oft-quoted evidence has been accurately reported, it is not representative and therefore should not be used to generalise from. This is said to apply to the whole of the period under discussion, when Henry's forays into the detailed business of government were unsustained and were mainly restricted to foreign policy, thus leaving ample scope for his leading servants to exercise the major control of events. But the interpretation is most convincing when applied to the final months of the king's life.

In this process of re-evaluation, two previously shadowy figures have emerged as men of considerable political influence. They are Sir Anthony Denny and Sir William Paget. Denny has remained the less understood of the two. He was in charge of the king's Privy Chamber – those rooms where Henry spent much of his time during his last years, and to which others could only gain admittance with Denny's agreement. He was therefore able to control who had access to the king, especially during those long periods when Henry was depressed and was less likely to assert his wishes. It is clear that Denny used his power both to keep out those whom he did want to have an opportunity to influence the king, and, during their frequent conversations, to present Henry with the information he wanted him to know. It has not yet proved possible to reach a convincing assessment of the cumulative effect of Denny's exercise of his power, but it was clearly substantial.

More is known about Paget, although the evidence about him is open to several interpretations. He was Henry's Private Secretary (the post that had been used by Cromwell from which to build his power base) during these years and, somewhat similar to Denny, was able to control the flow of written information that reached the king. He was an unscrupulous self-seeker and was probably instrumental in deciding which of the factions should finally emerge triumphant. He could have sided with either group, but was seemingly made the best offer by Hertford, and therefore facilitated the victory of the 'progressives'. In this he was assisted by Denny, who was almost certainly also part of the plot. The vital controlling mechanism was Henry's last will and testament. It seems probable that Paget drew up the first (and uncontroversial) part of this with the king's knowledge in December 1546, and arranged for it to be witnessed at this stage – the witnesses signing where plenty of space was left for further additions to be made. The details about the Regency Council were then added when the king was sufficiently near to death not to be able to do anything to alter them. Close examination of the relevant wording shows that, with Norfolk in the Tower awaiting execution and Gardiner excluded from court in disgrace for so-say failing to accept the king's instruction on the exchange of some diocesan land, the 'progressives' would be able to dominate the Council and would be able to utilise a loop-hole whereby Hertford would be able to exercise virtually full monarchical power. It was not even necessary for Henry to sign the will himself because Denny had control of the 'dry stamp' that for the past year had stood in place of the weakening king's actual mark. Although this version of events will never be able to be proved beyond doubt, it does ring the truest of all the scenarios so far offered by researchers. Thus there is room to believe that the wicked old tyrant of tradition was frequently (especially latterly) a pathetic old man who was shamelessly exploited by those who were entrusted to serve him.

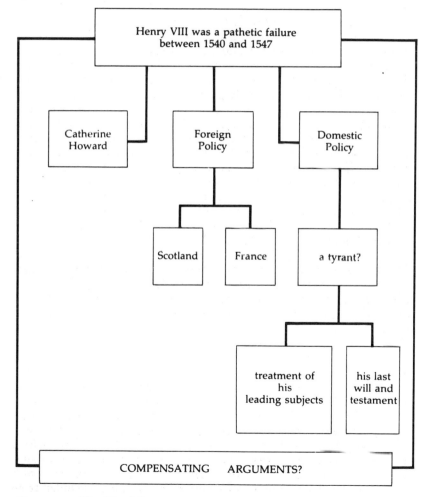

Summary – The Final Stage

As neither the 'orthodox' nor the 'revisionist' picture is very flattering to Henry VIII, it is difficult to escape the conclusion that the final stages of the king's life were very damaging in one form or another to his reputation. It was undoubtedly a tragedy that a reign that had begun with such high expectations should have ended in such political squalor. It will, of course, be for each reader to decide where, if anywhere, our sympathies should lie.

Making notes on 'The Final Stage'

This chapter has done two things. It has presented at some length the orthodox interpretation of the last years of Henry VIII as being a period of decline in English politics. It has also discussed some ways in which it might be valid to qualify the traditional version of events – the revisionist approach.

There are three things for you now to do.

1. You need to make sure that you understand the traditional interpretation and remember the major features of the evidence that has been used to support it. In doing this you are not expected to exercise your independence of thinking. Your aim should be to record the arguments advanced by others. The easiest way to do this is probably to make your notes using the headings and sub-headings that appear on pages 114–27.

2. You need to decide how far you accept the amendments to the traditional view, as discussed in section 5. Your notes on this section should be of a different kind to those on the earlier sections of the chapter. Here you should record your own conclusions, having thought through the arguments presented and having decided what your opinion is. In each case, it would be helpful to explain briefly why you have come to the opinion you have.

3. Once you have made your notes on the chapter, you need to consider how the conclusions you have come to influence your opinion about the character and personality of Henry VIII. Hopefully, this is one of the issues you have had at the forefront of your mind during your work on most of the book. Now is possibly the best time to come to some tentative final conclusions on this issue.

Answering essay questions on 'The Final Stage'

Sometimes examiners expect you to treat the subject matter of this chapter as a self-contained topic. But sometimes they expect you to link it with the events that either preceded or followed it. Most commonly, you will be asked to write about Henry's final years in the context of the 'mid-Tudor crisis' that some historians have seen it as precipitating. In order to answer such questions successfully you will need to know a fair amount about the whole of the period 1540–58. If you study *Edward VI and Mary: A Mid-Tudor Crisis?* in this series, you should be well equipped to tackle such questions.

Study the following questions, which are restricted to the reign of Henry VIII:

1. 'The final years of Henry VIII's life were a disaster for both England and its monarchy.' Discuss.
2. Assess the success of Henry VIII's dealings with France.
3. Why were the last seven years of Henry VIII's reign so unsuccessful?
4. What were the aims of England's foreign policy in the years 1509 to 1547?
5. Why were Henry VIII's matrimonial affairs generally so unsuccessful?
6. How far was Henry VIII in charge of affairs in England between the fall of Thomas Cromwell in 1540 and his own death in 1547?

If you carried out the tasks listed on page 92, you will already be experienced in ranking questions in what you consider to be their order of difficulty. Which do you think is the easiest of the six questions listed above? Why? What danger should you avoid if you were writing an essay to answer it?

Questions 3 and 5 share similarities in the way they are worded. But their most important similarity is in the nature of the assumptions they make. What is this similarity? In what way would this feature of the questions affect the way in which you answered it?

Question 2 suggests the need to link the contents of this chapter with those of chapter 3. This might best be done by the compilation of a 'foreign affairs date chart'. The wording of this question is also a reminder of the need to specify the criteria you are using when making an historical judgement. What criteria would you use when making your judgements in answer to this question?

Source-based questions on 'The Final Stage'

1 Henry VIII in 1544
Carefully study the portrait of Henry VIII in 1544 reproduced on page 115. Answer the following questions.
a) Identify the aspects of this portrait that show Henry in an unflattering light. (*5 marks*)

b) What is the significance of the presence of the *fleurs de lis* in Henry's coat of arms (top left of portrait)? *(2 marks)*
c) What can be deduced about Henry's perception of himself at this time that he allowed himself to be portrayed in this manner? *(5 marks)*
d) With what justification have some historians claimed that this portrait typifies the final stage of Henry's reign? *(7 marks)*

CHAPTER 8

Conclusion

1 Assessing Henry the King

When Henry died it seemed as if his reign had been a failure. Not only had his youthful dream of himself as a valiant knight winning momentous victories against the French not materialised, but his deep-felt desire to leave behind him an adult male heir with an inheritance of a secure and prosperous kingdom had not been achieved. The picture seemed very bleak. His only surviving son was nine-years-old and sickly. The monarchy was nearly bankrupt, the huge wealth acquired from the monasteries having been mostly squandered on futile wars. An uneasy peace with France was likely to break down at any moment, and the Scots were poised to take advantage of any political weakness south of the border. Religious discord was rife in many parts of the country, with numerous Protestants and reformers prepared to go to any lengths to overturn the conservative reaction that the final years of the old king's reign had witnessed. And, almost worst of all, the élite classes upon whom political and social stability rested were disunited over almost every element of government policy. It is no wonder that some historians have seen the situation on Henry's death to have been a recipe for disaster.

Yet the worst did not happen. Edward's succession was unchallenged, the country was not invaded, and law and order was maintained in most places on most occasions. The prophets of doom were to be disappointed. So had Henry been such a failure after all? The answer, of course, depends on the criteria one uses to make such a judgement.

The historians who belong to the whig tradition automatically look for 'progress' when they assess the success of any ruler. They are concerned to see whether an office-holder left the situation any more 'advanced' (which normally means nearer to the present state of affairs) than when he or she took charge. In Henry's case this frequently takes the form of a consideration whether the English state was any more modern in 1547 than it had been in 1509. If any part of the main Elton thesis is accepted, then, of course, the answer must be that it was, and that something of considerable significance was achieved during Henry's reign. However, it will be remembered (from chapter 6) that the current orthodoxy is that Elton's theses are, at best, unproven, and that it would be dangerous to place too much reliance on them. So are there other ways in which the English state could be thought to have progressed under Henry VIII?

It used to be widely accepted that the England inherited by Edward VI was markedly more united and independent than the state of which his father had become the head on the death of Henry VII. The case seemed almost self-evident. The 'liberties' in which the king's authority was not recognised in legal or administrative affairs – primarily the bishopric of Durham and the lordships of the Welsh Marches – had been brought within the mainstream of the English system. The whole of Wales was in essence made a part of England, (rather than being treated as a conquered territory), while Ireland was more firmly tied to the English crown when (in 1541) Henry was declared to be its king, rather than its lord. The previous title had been considered to be somewhat indefinite and to seem to depend upon a papal grant of authority. But most striking of all was the fact that the crown no longer shared sovereignty within its territories with a Church (with its own legal system as well as its sanctuaries in which the king's writ did not run) which was controlled by a foreign ruler (the Pope) as far as ultimate decision-making was concerned. Thus England became 'an empire sufficient unto itself', with the state being the final arbiter in all matters, and with the people thinking of themselves in increasingly insular and patriotic terms. The English nation-state had truly emerged.

However, this seemingly convincing case has been seriously undermined by detractors over many years and on several fronts. It has been argued that what appeared to be dramatic changes actually altered very little in practice: that Wales and the former liberties continued to be governed much as before; that the alteration of the Irish title was no more than a legal nicety to prevent successful challenges in the courts to the extinguishing of papal authority there; that the destruction of the Church's parallel legal system was only the ending of an arrangement that was never more than a minor inconvenience to the government; and that papal authority in England was of minimal importance, except for the brief period during which Wolsey, by the use of his legatine powers, chose to make it otherwise. Another line of attack had been to show that, on the one hand, the growth of English nationalism was well under way in the fifteenth century and therefore cannot have been a result of events in Henry's reign, and on the other hand that the 'flowering' of the English nation state did not take place until Henry had been dead for several decades and, therefore, was unlikely to have been caused by changes brought about under his authority. Although many current authorities on the subject have sympathy for these 'revisionist' interpretations, it is possible that the fashion for downgrading the changes brought about in the 1530s by suggesting that they were no more than modest steps in the very long-term development of the modern British state has been taken too far. There is still plenty of evidence that has not yet been discredited available to support the view that changes of fundamental importance took place in the nature of the English state while Henry VIII was king – even if some of them took a long time to become effective, and if it is impossible to prove that they were part of a consciously conceived plan. The 'historical pendulum' may yet swing again.

* Many of the historians who have consciously turned their backs on the whig emphasis on 'progress', still choose to assess success using criteria such as 'long-term effects' (which can end up seeming very similar to 'progress'). Henry VIII has generally received a low rating when the question has been, 'What were his lasting achievements?'. Commentators who dismiss the various 'changes in the nature of government or of the state' arguments have frequently been at a loss to identify anything of significant value that Henry left behind him. This is not surprising as – despite his periodic obsession with ensuring the future of his dynasty – Henry was essentially a 'man for the moment' rather than 'a builder for the future'. Although he was worried from time to time about the judgement that posterity might make of him, he was almost always much more concerned about what his contemporaries were thinking. He was not the type of man who would have exchanged (even had it been possible) fame during his own lifetime for positive coverage in the histories of the future. Thus the 'lasting achievements' question would not have seemed awfully relevant to him.

There are those writers who consider that the only valid historical assessments about individuals are those based on either the standards of their time or the goals that they set themselves. When such criteria are used it is possible to identify substantial areas of success for Henry VIII. Both the king himself and the orthodoxy of his time expected monarchs to be majestic. And that Henry indisputably was – even if some commentators would feel compelled to qualify the adjective with adverbs such as 'grotesquely'. It is true that some of the king's reputation for 'majesty' was created by good public relations work, as he was, for example, the first English monarch to arrange for copies of his portraits to be made on a sufficient scale for even those members of the élite who never came to court to be able to see how splendid he looked. But there was also plenty of substance to his reputation. Not only were there the high points, such as the Field of Cloth of Gold in 1520, but there was also the routine reception of guests at his court (especially of groups of foreign envoys) which were internationally renowned for their extravagance and splendour – not least for the fine gifts that visitors took away with them. Yet Henry did not adopt the seemingly obvious policy of taking his court to the people. This was a strategy that his daughter, Elizabeth I, was to develop with considerable effect, but her father only made the effort once. This was his long-promised and frequently postponed progress through the midlands to York in 1541, which was a resounding success in terms of the awe that was created in many of his subjects to the north of his normal hunting territories in the Home Counties.

Nor was Henry's success in creating a reputation for majesty all window-dressing. It had important political implications. For most of the middle ages the English king had in practice, as well as in theory, been *primus inter pares* (the first among equals). Although kings had long begun the process of distancing themselves from their leading nobles by 1509, it was during the reign of Henry VIII that the development became virtually irreversible. The Duke of Buckingham and the socially superior members of the Pilgrimage of Grace were almost the last Englishmen for more than a century to challenge (even by implication) the concept that the monarch was very much alone at the head of the nation's political and social hierarchies. The pre-eminence of the crown became the generally held orthodoxy during the years after 1509 largely because of what Henry did and the way in which he did it.

Henry had an eye for a fine house in a good position. By the time he died he possessed 55 of them, forming a 'collection' of impressive proportions and quality. He had acquired them in a variety of ways. Some were inherited, but the majority came from subjects who exhibited no desire to be rid of them. The most frequently adopted procedure was for Henry to suggest to the owner of a property he coveted that an exchange of houses might take place. It was very unusual for such a proposal to be declined. It is thought that Stephen Gardiner, the 'brains' of the conservative court faction, fell from favour in the final years of the king's reign largely because he raised objections to a patently unequal exchange that Henry wished to make involving a property that was under Gardiner's care as Bishop of Winchester. Certainly, Wolsey understood the rules of the game more clearly, and realised that there was nothing he could do to prevent his master taking possession of Hampton Court once his heart was set on doing so. Henry soon lost interest in many of the prizes he acquired – but not in all of them. In his later years he devoted much time, energy and money to developing one of them (Nonsuch Palace in Surrey) into an edifice that would most strikingly represent the glory of the English crown. Historians have generally been ungenerous in their assessments of his efforts, often unreasonably so. Possibly it has been too much of a temptation to use the fact that nothing now remains of the endeavour (the palace having been totally destroyed by fire later in the century) as symbolic of the reign of a man whom many have wished to criticise for leaving little of permanence behind him.

Yet, despite the fine reputation he had established for the majesty of his kingship, Henry died a very disappointed man. Not only was his son and heir a minor, but he had also failed to win the resounding military victories against the French upon which he had set his heart as a youth. That this aspiration stayed with him throughout his life seems to be proved by his insistence not only on going to war again in 1544 but also in leading his army in person against all the advice he was given (over 30 years after his first campaign in northern France). Although much was made of the capture of Boulogne in this latter excursion, he well knew that it was not another Agincourt, which it had always been his ambition to emulate. However, it may be unfair to assess Henry's achievements merely using the criterion of the goals he set himself. Perhaps it would be more valid to assess his success in terms of what was possible. If this approach is adopted, the verdict on him can be even more positive – once he has been criticised for setting himself unrealistic goals. It was widely accepted in western Europe during the 1520s and 1530s that there were three leading players in international affairs – Charles V, Francis I and Henry VIII. This, in itself, was a remarkable achievement for Henry, considering the relative resources at the three men's disposal. England had a population only about a tenth the size of that of Charles's domains and about a seventh the size of Francis's. Henry's income was in a roughly similar proportion. Hence, for England to have been thought of as being in the same 'league' as the other two major powers was a very positive reflection on the way in which Henry was able to project his own and his kingdom's strength.

2 Assessing Henry the Man

If you have read the whole (or even the major part) of this book, you will already have become aware of the controversy that exists about the personality and character of Henry VIII, and you may already have made up your mind about which interpretation seems the more convincing. If you are particularly perceptive you may even have identified the blend of ideas that the current author favours. However, it is important to keep in the forefront of your mind that none of the cases would satisfy a judge in a court of law. Little, and certainly not a complete interpretation, has been established 'beyond reasonable doubt'. To continue the metaphor, 'the jury is still out', and it is likely to be so for a long time, if not for ever. But this should not prevent each person who studies the period from reaching a tentative conclusion on the issue: in fact, it is an open invitation to do so. Nor should it be imagined that the only possibilities are the 'packages' that were outlined in chapters 1 and 2. If a mix of ideas that forms a new package seems to offer the most coherent explanation, then there is every reason to adopt it as a 'for the time being' stance.

However, there seems to be little likelihood that a choice within the 'essentially strong or good: essentially weak or bad' dichotomy can be completely avoided. But there is no need to choose one of the more extreme overall assessments. Henry has been described as 'the Stalin of the Tudor period' and as 'the wisest king that England ever had'. Neither assessment appears to have much to recommend it. With such a range of qualifying factors 'on offer', it would only be the relatively unthinking student who would decide on such a stark assessment. Was he really as cruel as members of the 'weak' school have often made out? Certainly, he was not consistently so. He was genuinely upset (and for a prolonged period) when Catherine Howard's indiscretions meant that his honour dictated that he must allow her to be executed, while the vengeance wreaked against the Pilgrims in 1536–7 could easily have been much more extensive. And could he have been as unscrupulous as the 'strong' supporters have sometimes argued? If he was, it is amazing that he chose to face the agonies of the long battle to obtain the annulment of his marriage to Catherine of Aragon when a poisoner could have readily been employed to achieve a speedy and certain result.

These questions, together with the comments made in response to them, possibly offer a clue to the most effective way for the non-research historian to arrive at a reasonable independent judgement about the personality and character of Henry VIII. Elton long ago argued that in the study of Henrician England we should often be guided as much by the lack of a particular type of evidence as by the existence of facts that support a favoured interpretation. So the most useful type of question to ask in deciding one's stance on the 'What sort of person was Henry VIII?' issue may well be 'If Henry was x, then would not he have done y?'.

Whether or not this is so, at least one certainty remains. The issue has exercised great fascination and excited strong emotions for a very long time, and there is every reason to think that it will continue to do so. But what is especially pleasing is that it is a controversy in which we can all legitimately join. And once the 'bug' has been caught it is unlikely ever to be lost.

Working on the Conclusion

This is not a chapter on which you should make notes as if you were an outside observer. Now you must get onto the 'inside'. If you have not already done so, you have decisions to make on two sets of issues.

1. Assessing Henry VIII's success or failure as King of England, and
2. Assessing Henry VIII's personality and character.

In both cases you must decide on the criteria you will use. Unless you do this you are likely to end up in a muddle.

You may come to the conclusion that several sets of criteria are historically equally valid, although in different ways. This can be an acceptable position to take up. But you must be clear in your own mind which set you are using at any one time (and, preferably, why). Equally, it is also allowable to decide that only one set of criteria is defensible, given the values that you hold. In that case, of course, you should be prepared to justify your choice.

Once you have chosen your criteria, the process of reaching your judgement is relatively straightforward, although it may involve you in a large amount of work. You will need to refer back to the notes you made on the earlier chapters to refresh your memory on the facts you learnt and the conclusions you reached on each issue. Rather than doing this 'cold', it will probably be more beneficial to skim through your notes several times. Each time you should have a very specific question in mind, and your aim should be to locate ideas and information that help to answer it.

For example, if you have decided that the best way in which to judge a ruler's success or failure is to assess the extent to which he improved the lot of his subjects, your first question might be, 'In what ways did the actions of Henry VIII improve conditions for the people of England during his reign?'. You may think that the wording of this question is too restrictive. If you do, what question would you use to replace it? What question would you pose for a second skim through of your notes?

The paragraphs above have been written with students who are nearing the end of their course in mind. However, you may still be near the beginning of your advanced studies. In that case, you may not yet be ready to tackle the tasks suggested in this section, and it may be best to do nothing more at this stage. But when the time is right, the more you are able to think about the issues raised in this volume (rather than just learning the facts it contains), the greater will be your overall progress in the subject. And if the prospect daunts you somewhat, it is worth remembering that for most people thinking about issues is much harder than learning the facts. Both are important in the study of history, but it is the former that is likely to do you by far the most good. Maybe the people are right who claim that thinking through an issue is a painfully acquired capability: they are certainly correct in maintaining that the effort involved in acquiring the skill is normally repaid many times over during the average person's life!

Chronological Table

1472/3	Thomas Wolsey born.
1485	Henry VII became king after his victory in the battle of Bosworth.
	? Thomas Cromwell born.
1491	28 June, Henry VIII born at Greenwich Palace.
1501	Arthur and Catherine of Aragon married.
1502	Arthur died.
1509	21 April, Henry VII died.
	11 June, wedding of Henry VIII and Catherine of Aragon.
	23 June, Henry VIII's coronation.
1510	March, truce with France renewed, probably against Henry's wishes.
1512	England joined Spain in a new alliance against France, but a campaign in association with Ferdinand was a disaster. The army sent to Spain to take part in a joint attack on France achieved nothing.
1513	April, the Emperor joined an alliance of England, Spain and the Papacy against France. (Spain deserted almost immediately.)
	30 June, Henry joined the Emperor (Maximilian I) in France.
	16 August, Battle of the Spurs, a notional English victory.
	24 August, Thérouanne taken. Immediately sacked by the Emperor.
	9 September, an English army, under the Earl of Surrey, defeated the Scots at Flodden.
	23 September, Tournai taken.
1514	August, Henry made peace with France after all his allies had deserted him.
1515	January, accession of Francis I as King of France.
1516	February, Mary (Catherine of Aragon's only child to survive) born. She reigned as Mary I from 1553 to 1558.
1518	Treaty of London. Henry's and Wolsey's attempt to ensure a general peace.
1519	Charles V elected Holy Roman Emperor (in addition to his existing Habsburg, Burgundian and Spanish inheritances).
1520	May, Henry met Charles V in England.
	June, Henry and the English court met Francis I and the French court at the Field of Cloth of Gold outside Calais.
	July, Henry met Charles V at Calais.
1521	May, execution of the Duke of Buckingham.

August, Wolsey visited Charles V at Bruges. Agreement reached (confirmed and extended in June 1522) for a joint invasion of France, each with an army of 40,000 men.

1523   August, an English army of 10,000 under the Duke of Suffolk landed at Calais. Siege of Boulogne abandoned in order to make an attack on Paris. This became bogged down in the winter mud and was abandoned.

1525   14 February, Battle of Pavia. French defeated by an Imperial army, Francis I captured, and Richard de la Pole killed.

March, Amicable Grant commissioned to pay for an intended invasion of France. Abandoned because of opposition to its collection.

30 August, Henry made peace with France.

1527   Henry committed himself to Anne Boleyn and decided to seek an annulment of his marriage to Catherine of Aragon.

April, offensive alliance against Charles V signed with France.

1528   January, England and France declared war on Charles V.

1529   5 August, Treaty of Cambrai making peace between Charles V and Francis I.

October, Wolsey dismissed.

1530   29 November, Wolsey died at Leicester.

1533   25 January, Henry and Anne Boleyn married secretly.

31 May, Anne Boleyn crowned queen.

7 September, Elizabeth born. She later reigned as Elizabeth I (1558–1603).

Thomas Cromwell 'emerges' as Henry's leading minister.

1536   7 January, Catherine of Aragon died.

19 May, Anne Boleyn executed.

30 May, Henry married Jane Seymour.

2–18 October, the Lincolnshire Uprising.

8 October, Pilgrimage of Grace began in Yorkshire, led by Robert Aske.

1537   12 October, Jane Seymour gave birth to Edward and died twelve days later. He later reigned as Edward VI (1547–53).

1538   Papal bull of deprivation deposing Henry VIII. Fear of French invasion at its height.

1538/9   Leading members of the White Rose Party executed.

1540   6 January, Henry married Anne of Cleves. Marriage not consummated. Divorce arranged within 6 months.

10 June, Thomas Cromwell arrested.

28 July, Thomas Cromwell executed. Henry married Catherine Howard.

1541   Henry's progress in the North.

Henry assumed the title 'King of Ireland'.

1542   13 February, Catherine Howard executed.

	Henry declared war on Scotland.
	25 November, an English army defeated a Scottish army at the battle of Solway Moss.
	14 December, James V of Scotland died, leaving the infant Mary as his heir.
1543	1 July, Treaty of Greenwich signed with Scotland. The Scots rejected it in December.
	12 July, Henry married Catherine Parr.
	Henry declared war on France.
1544	English invasion and devastation of southern Scotland by Edward Seymour in an attempt to remove the Scottish threat while France was invaded.
	14 September, Boulogne taken by an English army.
1545	French attempt to invade England failed without there being a major engagement.
1546	June, peace between England and France signed at Ardres – France abandoned the Scots.
1547	28 January, Henry died. His reign had lasted 37 years and 8 months.

(This Chronological Table omits all events that are primarily 'religious' affairs. These may be found in *Henry VIII and the Reformation in England* in this series.)

Acknowledgements

The Publishers would like to thank the following for permission to reproduce material in this volume:
Cambridge University Press, for the extracts from G R Elton *The Tudor Revolution in Government* (Cambridge University Press, 1953).

The Publishers would also like to thank the following for permission to reproduce copyright illustrations:
Bodleian Library, p57; HM the Queen, p51; Hulton Picture Library p115; National Portrait Gallery pp10, 12, 108; The Walker Art Gallery, cover.

Every effort has been made to trace and acknowledge ownership of copyright. The Publishers will be glad to make suitable arrangements with any copyright holders whom it has not been possible to contact.

Further Reading

1 Textbooks

It would be time well spent if you were rapidly to read the relevant chapters of two general textbooks covering the whole of the Tudor period (i.e., not making detailed notes as you do so). The aim should be to spot the general interpretations supported by the authors. The most accessible of the modern texts, giving up-to-date interpretations on many of the relevant issues, is

John Guy, *Tudor England* (O.U.P 1988).

A considerable contrast would be provided by the most stimulating text of the previous generation

G. R. Elton, *England under the Tudors* (Methuen 1955).

A productive exercise would be to make a list of the major political issues of the period (as you understand them) and then briefly to note the 'line' taken by Guy and Elton on each of them. An absence of coverage by one or other of the books might provoke interesting ideas about the changing *foci* of interest among historians of the topic.

2 Biographies

There are dozens of widely available biographies of the major characters of the period. But one stands head and shoulders above the others in terms of its usefulness to students studying the topic at an advanced level. This is

J. J. Scarisbrick, *Henry VIII* (Methuen 1968).

This volume has done more than any other to shape a whole generation of writers' perceptions of Henry's reign and it has established a new orthodoxy about the period. Any student taking the study of the topic at all seriously should read as much of this book as time permits.

Two other biographies are outstanding examples of their kind and a reading of part of each of them would do much to 'round out' your understanding of the period.

E. W. Ives, *Anne Boleyn* (Blackwell 1986)

is a proof that a biography written according to the highest academic standards can also be made interesting to the general public. In it the reader is shown the steps by which an experienced professional historian pieces together an account from evidence that is frequently very incomplete and/or unreliable. It provides a splendid case study of the art of the historian.

L. B. Smith, *Henry VIII: The Mask of Royalty* (London 1971)

is very different. Although the processes gone through by the historian are largely hidden, the fact that the author has developed a wide-ranging and perceptive understanding of the period constantly shines through. Interesting insights are to be found on almost every page, so that even a brief dipping into it can be a rewarding experience.

Unfortunately there are no works on Henry's two great ministers (Wolsey and Cromwell) that can be recommended at this level.

Peter Gwyn, *The King's Cardinal: The Rise and Fall of Thomas Wolsey* (Barrie & Jenkins 1990)

is a 650 page long mine of information, but it is likely only to interest the reader who has already become a Wolsey-buff. Sir Geoffrey Elton's extensive writings on Cromwell are well worth reading for studies to degree level, but are probably too demanding and diffuse for other students.

3 Specialist Studies

Nearly all of the many specialist works on aspects of the politics of the Henrician age are too detailed for all but the dedicated reader. However, there is a readable volume on foreign affairs which, although somewhat dated, is one of the few places where most of the relevant material can be found gathered together. This is

R. B. Wernham, *Before the Armada: the Growth of English Foreign Policy 1485–1558* (Jonathan Cape 1966).

A highly successful attempt by one of the leading historians of the period to make the subject accessible to a wide public is

David Starkey, *The Reign of Henry VIII: Personalities & Politics* (George Philip 1985).

It is an easy and interesting read, especially for those who have already established the 'shape' of the topic in their minds. Significant issues are raised that are normally only discussed in much more daunting volumes.

Students who wish to track down more specialist works can most effectively start to do so via the bibliography in Guy's volume.

Index

Readers seeking a specific piece of information might find it helpful to consult the table of *Contents* and the *Chronological Table* as well as this brief *Index*.

The South East Essex
College of Arts & Technology
Carnarvon Road, Southend-on-Sea, Essex SS2 6LS
Phone 0702 220400 Fax 0702 432320 Minicom 0702 220642